Teaching Science in the Primary Classroom: A practical guide

By
Hellen Ward, Judith Roden, Claire Hewlett and Julie Foreman

Paul Chapman Publishing

First published 2005

Reprinted 2005, 2006 (twice)

Paul Chapman Publishing
A SAGE Publications Company
1 Oliver's Yard
55 City Road
London EC1Y 1SP

SAGE Publications Inc.
2455 Teller Road
Thousand Oaks, California 91320

SAGE Publications India Pvt Ltd
B-42, Panchsheel Enclave
New Delhi 110 017

British Library Cataloguing in Publication Data
A catalogue record for this book is available from the British Library

ISBN-10 1-4129-0340-8   ISBN-13 978-1-4129-0340-0
ISBN-10 1-4129-0341-6 (pbk)   ISBN-13 978-1-4129-0341-7 (pbk)

Library of Congress Control Number: 2004115096

Typeset by Pantek Arts Ltd, Maidstone, Kent
Printed in Great Britain by T.J. International, Padstow, Cornwall

Contents

Foreword

At last a book that clearly focuses on the promotion and development of science learning from the Foundation Stage to Key Stage 2. The four authors have extensive experience in initial teacher education and in primary schooling and this is evident in the emphasis on practical examples and evidence-based guidance.

Based in initial teacher education the authors have based much of the content on recent and relevant research, with a particular aim of making the scientific content lively, contemporary and fun.

Initial teacher education students, teachers and science leaders/co-ordinators will find the book accessible, yet challenging. The examples and case studies are current and designed to help teachers make science learning active and creative.

I believe that readers will welcome the assistance with planning, process skills and assessment, but more crucially will see how the range of components in the book contribute to science learning in the primary school.

Professor Hugh Lawlor
Director of AstraZeneca Science Teaching Trust
and DfES Adviser

Acknowledgements

We would like to thank the many people who have contributed to this book, both directly and indirectly, including colleagues, both past and present, who have helped to shape the science courses upon which this book is based.

More specifically, we owe many thanks to our primary science technician, Hugh Ritchie who has provided much encouragement and essential support during the preparation of this book. He has been calming and reassuring when surrounded by the hectic nature of life at Canterbury Christ Church University College. We are indebted to him for his work in producing many of the photographs included in this book. Without Hugh, the book may never have made it into print. We would also like to thank Keith Remnant and Paddy Grinter for their skills in proofreading and editing and Kerry for her typing skills and patience in coping with numerous changes.

Thanks are due to Peter Ellse and the staff of TTS for equipment and support.

Thanks are also due to the many ex-students and teachers, in the institutions in which we have worked, who have provided the inspiration and opportunities for us to develop our ideas about teaching science over the years. In particular we would like to thank the head teachers, teachers and pupils of the following schools:

Bobbing Village School, Kent
Davigdor Infant School, Brighton and Hove, West Sussex
Elphinstone County Primary School, Hastings, East Sussex
Eythorne and Elvington Primary School, Kent
Graveney Primary School, Graveney, Kent
Hollington County Primary School, Hastings, East Sussex
Morehall Primary School, Folkestone, Kent
Park Wood Junior School, Rainham, Medway
Senacre Wood Primary School, Maidstone, Kent
St Benedict's RC Primary School, Chatham, Medway
Whitstable Junior School, Kent

Finally we would like to thank our long-suffering families, particularly our partners and husbands who share our enthusiasm for our work with student teachers, teachers and pupils.

About the Authors

Hellen Ward is primarily interested in teaching and learning especially in the areas of science and assessment. She is a well-respected and active member of both ASE and AAIA. In addition to her role at Canterbury Christ Church University College she works with Local Education Authorities, schools, organisations and companies. This work has led to a number of publications, interactive work for websites and articles on primary science education. Hellen is frequently asked to contribute to conference programmes making presentations or running workshops. Her research interest is linked to pupils' attitudes to science education.

Judith Roden is an experienced teacher of science in all phases of education. She is currently a Principal Lecturer working in the Faculty of Education, where her main area of work is primary science education. She has written, chapters for a number of books, articles and has made conference presentations. Judith has recently been the project director of University College's AstraZeneca Science Teaching Trust funded school-based project that focused on the whole school development of science in thirty-six primary schools in Kent and Medway.

Claire Hewlett has twelve years experience teaching in primary schools in East Kent. She spent five years as a science co-ordinator in her last post, prior to becoming a Headteacher. Claire has been a senior lecturer within the Department of Education for the past four years where she works alongside other members of the primary team teaching on both the undergraduate and PGCE programmes. She is particularly interested in how cross curricular links can be made between science and other curriculum areas, particularly with literacy. Claire also co-ordinates the Year 3 undergraduate programme.

Julie Foreman is an experienced teacher of science in primary education. She is currently a Senior Lecturer working in the Faculty of Education, where her main area of work is primary science education, working with a range of students including undergraduates, postgraduates and specialist teacher assistants. Julie has recently been a tutor on the University College's AstraZeneca Science Teaching Trust funded school-based project that focused on the whole school development of science in thirty-six primary schools in Kent and Medway, from which she has undertaken research and conference presentations. Her further areas of research have focused upon children's investigative science and the use of role-play to stimulate and develop children's understanding of scientific concepts.

CHAPTER 1

What is Science?

Judith Roden and Hellen Ward

Introduction

This chapter will explore the reasons why science is important and why it should be taught in the primary school. Initially it will outline the nature of science and the development of scientific ideas. Drawing on recent research into children's attitudes towards science, the focus will be on science as a creative activity. Later it will provide examples of resources that can be used at different key stages to develop creative science practically. Additionally, it will explore the importance of ideas and evidence, starting with pupils' ideas and collecting data that will help them to develop respect for evidence. It will also explore the value of group work in science within the primary class-room, i.e. it will take a wider look at the social aspects of science as a collaborative activity and its importance in the development of key learning skills. These features will be interwoven to demonstrate that it is the development of pupil attitudes towards science that impacts on their learning.

Why Science Is Important

Science education is a matter of crucial importance to the UK, both for the future generations of scientists, engineers and technologists and for the wider public. Science and technology are essential for our economic competitiveness, and to our quality of life, and lie at the heart of our history and culture. (Science and Technology Committee, 2002, Introduction, p. 1)

Although important, the major purpose of science education is not only to produce well-qualified scientists who will be the researchers of tomorrow, but also to produce well-balanced individual members of society. The needs of the individual and society are obviously closely linked. Both for the future well-being of individuals and of society as a whole, it is important that there is a creative and scientifically literate population. Adults need to be scientifically literate in the immediate future because they will need to have a range of skills, aptitudes and abilities to enable them take up the employment opportunities of the future. It is likely that individuals may well have to change their type of employment, repeatedly, to meet the challenges of a rapidly changing technological society.

In the developed countries, in recent years, there has been a move away from the heavy and light engineering and manufacturing base of the past. There is now a trend for this type of enterprise to take place in the developing world where labour costs are generally much cheaper.

More typically, today and increasingly, employment in the developed countries relates to the service industries including financial services. Now and in the future, another major opportunity for employment in developed countries is the creation and design of innovative new products for manufacture in the developing countries. Furthermore, individuals will need to be able to communicate their ideas to others. It is crucial to the future of the British economy, therefore, for individuals to have the creative, innovative and communicative skills introduced to them at the primary level and developed throughout the education system. Future adults will also need an understanding of science to enable them to make informed decisions about important issues related to science in society, e.g. genetically modified crops, human cloning, nuclear power, wind turbines, global warming, etc.

The Four Threads of Science

Historically, science has had two aspects: first, a body of knowledge and, secondly, a way of working. The two aspects are totally and inextricably linked. Whenever scientists work, they find out about the world using aspects of scientific method. Similarly, pre-school children find out about the world using the same basic methods. Although the level of sophistication and the tools used in their tasks will be different, basically both scientists and pupils find out about the world using the same processes. For many years, in theory, if not always in popular practice, one of the principle aims of science education has been to develop pupils' understanding through the use of scientific approaches.

Being scientific also involves the development of concepts like electricity or change or movement, etc. There is a strong relationship between pupils' use of scientific method and the development of scientific understanding. Furthermore, developments in both aspects of science are strongly influenced by, and rely upon, scientists' and pupils' attitudes towards science. The attitudes involved in 'being scientific', generally include curiosity, respect for evidence, willingness to tolerate uncertainty, creativity and inventiveness, open-mindedness, critical reflection, co-operation with others, sensitivity to living and non-living things and perseverance. Although, Johnson (1996) sees scientific development as a 'triple helix' with three threads, conceptual understanding, skills and attitudes all developing together to support later understanding, a further area is important in joining the strands together and this is the area of scientific procedures. Scientific procedures are different from skills and include the nature of science and the development of scientific ideas. These four threads are linked and are vital if science is to continue to have any relevance for the pupils in the twenty-first century. For without this breadth, science is a dry and limiting subject which fails to interest and excite, where the past trials and successes are reduced to a list of facts to be learnt and experiments to be conducted.

The Importance of Science in the Primary School

The place of science as a core subject in the primary curriculum can be justified in many ways, not least because science contributes to pupils' acquisition of key skills including thinking skills (Harlen, 2000a; 2000b). According to the National Curriculum (DfEE, 1999), science is about stimulating and exciting pupils' curiosity about the world around them: 'Science is an integral part of modern culture. It stretches the imagination and creativity of young people. Its challenges are quite enormous' (DfEE, 1999, p.78). Given this view, it is not surprising that the development of aspects of scientific skills can be identified in the *Curriculum Guidance for the Foundation Stage* within Knowledge and Understanding of the World and is promoted in both Key Stages 1 and 2 of the National Curriculum.

Fundamentally, throughout the Foundation Stage, Key Stages 1 and 2 and beyond, there is a gradual development of scientific knowledge and understanding, and when the development of scientific processes is fully incorporated into a child's programme of science it can help them to understand science better. The Qualification and Curriculum Authority (QCA) (2000, p.32) states that in order for children in the Foundation Stage to successfully develop their knowledge and understanding of the world, teachers need to provide: 'Activities based on first-hand experiences that encourage exploration, observation, problem solving, prediction, critical thinking, decision making and discussion' (QCA, 2000, p.82). A real challenge for the early years teacher and indeed all teachers!

The National Curriculum requires pupils to draw upon their everyday experiences and to 'use first hand information and simple information sources' (DfEE, 1999, p.78). The science curriculum (DfEE, 1999) separates science into four programmes of study. Essentially, these represent scientific enquiry (Sc1), life processes and living things (Sc2), materials and their properties (Sc3) and physical processes (Sc4). Although separate, there is much overlap between the four aspects and they should not be seen as totally discrete entities. In particular, scientific enquiry should permeate all other programmes of study. Consequently, science process skills feature largely in the curriculum and this should be, though often it is not, reflected in classroom practice. However, whilst the process skills are important, they are not the same as procedural understanding and this aspect needs to be incorporated explicitly into schools' science schemes of work.

Attitudes for learning science are also important and need consideration and development. Attitudes do not feature explicitly in the science National Curriculum 2000, however, they are important and, when considering a pupil's education holistically, cannot be ignored.

Overall, the development of understanding of science is dependent on all these aspects. Teachers need to weave a carpet of provision of science for primary aged pupils where knowledge and understanding develops alongside scientific procedures, skills and attitudes towards and in science.

Pupils' Attitudes towards Science

Research into pupils' attitudes towards science reveals that their attitudes are formed at an early age. Therefore, it is crucial to capture this natural interest in science and to capitalise upon pupils' experiences of finding out about the world through exploration. The aim of school science is to extend these opportunities rather than to limit the curriculum as seems to be the case today in some schools. The Acclaim Project (www.acclaimscientists.org.uk) interviewed eminent scientists engaged in current research and development in science. One of the most interesting findings related to the age at which the scientists decided that they had first became interested in science. Typical responses included:

'I don't remember when I was not interested in science.'

'I was interested in science from a very young age, perhaps 5 or 6.'

Whilst female scientists seemed to suggest they were older when their interest in science began, a common factor identified for all was the exposure to other people who had a passion for things scientific, i.e. a parent, relative or friend. Significantly, teachers and 'hands-on' experiences were both identified as factors that played an influential role in developing the scientists' interest in science. This concurs with views regularly expressed by practising and intending teachers whose own experiences in school science, both positive and negative, impact significantly on their long-term attitudes towards the subject.

Clearly, then, it is important for science to feature regularly throughout the primary years. However, it is important not only that it is included, but that it is of the right quality. The Her Majesty's Inspectorate (HMI) subject report for Primary Science (OfSTED/HMI, 2003) found that there had been a reduction in the time given to science and, particularly, for investigative work. Issues highlighted in Office for Standards in Education (OfSTED) reports and HMI publications regularly include the lack of, or poor quality of, science in primary schools.

Other research suggests that many pupils have poor attitudes towards learning in science at the primary level. Pollard and Triggs (2000) found that as the pupils in the sample grew older, science became one of three subjects least liked in the primary curriculum and that, by Year 5 and Year 6, pupils rarely nominated science as the subject most liked, favouring art and physical education instead. Pupils said they found science difficult and disliked both the amount of writing they had to do and the weight of information they had to learn. Girls consistently disliked science more than boys until Year 6 when antipathy was much more evenly divided between the sexes. Worryingly, findings suggested that as primary pupils grew older their awareness of learning processes in science declined rather than grew. For example, there was a decline in their awareness of science as an investigative activity because of the tightly framed subject-based and teacher-controlled curriculum (Pollard and Triggs, 2000, pp.87–98).

Pupils need to be provided both with the opportunity and the time to engage with the processes and the procedures of sciences in order to develop sound knowledge and understanding, and to develop more positive attitudes as a result.

The Importance of Group Work

Unlike many subjects of the primary curriculum, science provides the opportunity for working as a group rather than working independently within a group situation. Science enables pupils to be involved in group work where they have the opportunity to share ideas and co-operate with each other in collaborative practical activity. Research shows that pupils who work together learn more than when working alone. Sharing ideas and group work are also important to scientific activity. When asked what qualities were needed to solve a scientific problem, an eminent scientist replied:

The ability to ask the right question is very important...perseverance and deter-mination ... Lateral thinking is useful when a straightforward solution to the problem is not obvious. The ability to admit that the scientific evidence shows that your pet idea is wrong and someone else's idea is right is also important. Today, much science is done in teams, so the ability to work in a team is helpful. (www.acclaimscientists.org.uk)

Clearly these qualities are not exclusive to science and scientists and, therefore, the development of these qualities should be at the heart of education. However, being able to work as part of a group is needed if pupils' procedural under-standing and scientific attitudes are to be developed. Practical science provides many opportunities not only for the sharing and challenging of ideas amongst peers, but also for the development of group skills. The role of the teacher is crucial in this process: 'neglect of the process skills means that children have to take ideas as given by teacher or text book and there is a great deal of experi-ence that shows that this is unlikely to lead to understanding' (Sherrington, 1998, p.28). If the teacher always plans the investigation, providing only oppor-tunities for illustrative activities, i.e. those that illustrate a concept or scientific principle, the skill of planning will be lost.

Starting with the pupils' own ideas is important, as they need to develop their ideas progressively in a variety of topics throughout their primary years. Pupils need to be taught how to ask questions and find the answers using a wide range of approaches and, in doing so, to collect evidence. Approaching collected data with an open mind, trying to make sense of any developing patterns and draw-ing conclusions are activities that develop respect for evidence. Collaborative group work introduces pupils to the social aspects of science as well as provid-ing opportunities for the development of key learning skills. All these features are interwoven and support the development of pupil attitudes towards science, which have a major impact on learning.

The Nature of Scientific Ideas

The amount of scientific knowledge and understanding is immense and has been developed over thousands of years. Some original ideas have been chal-lenged over time, for example, that the earth is the centre of the universe and flat. Other ideas have been refined over time, for example the idea that the atom is composed of neutrons, electrons and protons. However, most of the ideas in science accepted as true today have one thing in common: that there is some evidence to support them. Conclusions have been drawn and have been communicated to others, which has resulted in the ideas being challenged and rejected or accepted. Pupils should develop an understanding of the ways in which facts have changed over time, and this aspect of science should be included in the teaching and learning approaches used in the primary school. If it is not, then science merely becomes a body of knowledge that has to be learnt, with no opportunities for a new slant or a creative response on behalf of the pupils. The focus on what is known rather than how it is known makes science sterile. Evaluating evidence is important in science and is also an important generic life skill. Open-mindedness and respect for evidence are important attitudes in science and important also to everyday life, i.e. making decisions based upon evidence rather than jumping to conclusions.

Enabling pupils to make the link between their ideas and the evidence for these can be encouraged through simple activities. A good activity to make explicit the need to look objectively and to respect evidence to support conclusions follows, starting with Figure 1.1.

Figure 1.1 *What ideas do this picture generate?*

Pupils can be asked to reveal the ideas they hold as a result of looking at the picture above. When shown this drawing recently, some pupils stated that they thought the drawings were of footprints. When asked why they thought this, it was clear that they had brought evidence from everyday life to their interpretation of the drawing, for example having seen birds' footprints in the snow. They also stated that one animal was bigger than the other, as evidenced by the size of the footprint, and that the animal with larger prints had claws. Whilst the smaller animal moved with both feet together, the larger footprints were made one at a time. An adult learner suggested that the small footprints were made by an animal with a small brain who had not evolved a brain big enough to have co-ordinated movement.

When more evidence (Figure 1.2) was presented, the pupils put forward ideas of a meeting between the two animals resulting in the smaller animal flying away, having a piggyback or coming to a 'sticky end'. The evidence that supported these ideas was gleaned and questions were asked which focused the pupils on what evidence explicitly supported their ideas and whether all ideas could be correct. In this case all ideas had merit, although pupils developed their 'pet idea' but it was not possible to discount the other views. In fact, there was no evidence to suggest that both footprints were made at the same time! Once the pupils realised that in this type of science lesson the expectation was for them to promote ideas, to discuss evidence and that their responses could be modified as more evidence came to light, they were ready and willing to use their enthusiasm and creativity in other activities.

Figure 1.2 *More evidence is provided; have the ideas changed?*

Everyday materials were used to link science to real life, that is, pupils were asked to apply this approach to a different, but everyday setting situation. A range of cans of proprietary soft drinks, i.e. a 'Coke', a 'diet Coke' and a 'Seven-up' and a tank of water were used to challenge pupils to provide ideas of what would happen when the cans were placed in water. Pupils used previous knowledge of floating and sinking to arrive at suggestions. Suggestions included 'Diet Coke will float as it is lighter' and 'They will all sink because they are heavy'. The cans were placed into the water one by one, with an opportunity for the pupils to observe what happen to each can, and pupils were asked if they would like to alter their ideas based on the new evidence. In the event, the 'Seven-up' sank, the 'Coke' floated just off the bottom and 'diet Coke' floated just below the surface, which resulted in amazement and quick suggestions as to why this might be. The pupils then had to think of ways to test out their ideas.

Suggested tests included weighing the cans, measuring the liquid, counting the number of bubbles in set amounts of each liquid and the use of secondary sources to research the composition of each liquid (for example, amount of sugar). One pupil suggested that if the cans had been placed in the tank in a different order a different result would have occurred! Highlighting pupils who require support or challenge is an additional advantage of working in this way. Although no writing was involved in the original part of the session, this did not make this activity less valuable. When the pupils tried out their tests they recorded their results and communicated their findings in poster form later in the week.

Challenging pupils to use their ideas and collect evidence can occur in most activities, but it requires changes to the way that science is delivered in some primary classrooms.

Tracks in everyday modern life provide as many challenges as using examples from pre-history. The tracks in Figure 1.3 were made on a beach in 2004. Looking at the tracks should provide some evidence as to the 'animals' that made the different tracks. This picture and others are also provided on a website (www.paulchapmanpublishing.co.uk\resources\ward.pdf) to download for use in the classroom, along with examples of pupils' work and the activities produced throughout this book. Enabling pupils to be creative just requires less teacher direction and an understanding that science can be fun.

Figure 1.3 *What made these tracks? For further examples and close ups, including what made these tracks, go to the website www.paulchapmanpublishing.co.uk\resources\ward.pdf*

Simple Starting Points for Interesting and Creative Activities

Initially, when asked to use a simple object as a starting point for creative science activities, practising teachers and students in training often state that they find this difficult and scary. However, when challenged to do so, they often provide a wealth of ideas for sharing with colleagues: 'At first I was really worried, I didn't know what I could choose, but when you think carefully, look in books and so on, it is so simple, isn't it!' (PGCE student, 2004).

Creative and interesting activities can be developed from many different, but simple starting points. Table 1.1 provides some suggestions for creative practical activities from starting points where the initial focus is on play, exploration and observation. Many of the activities can be approached at different key stages, but need to be tailored to meet the known needs of individuals and groups of pupils in the classroom. Teachers and other adults can start by presenting the object to the pupil, stepping back to observe what pupils notice, how they interact with the object(s) and noting what questions are asked. Differentiation is by outcome, as initially the pupils will approach each task with differing levels of skills and experience. It is found that younger pupils will approach objects in a different way to older pupils, with their approach based on trial and error. The expectation of older pupils is that they will apply a more systematic, logical approach to the activities, although this depends upon previous experiences and opportunities to work independently.

Resource	Creative practical activities
Digital camera close-up photographs of various objects, e.g. pineapple	Guess what the object is? Observational drawings of small parts of the object looking for detail. Pupils take close-up photographs and challenge others to identify them.
Eyes	Looking at each other's eyes. Noticing the different colours of eyes.Recording their friend's eyes using wool stuck on card. Covering eyes and observe change in pupils.
Baby teeth Toothbrush Toothpaste	Looking at different shapes of teeth and their function. Mixing toothpastes with water and observing how much foam occurs and whether all the toothpaste dissolves.
Looking at different animal bones	What animal did it come from? How do you know? What ways are they the same? What are the differences? Which bone might have been a mouse and which an elephant? Close observation using digital microscope.
Woolly jumper	Close observation of wool. Looking at where the wool comes from and how it is treated to become the jumper. Wool under the digital microscope.
Archimedes thermometer	Watching the liquid filled bulbs rise and fall with temperature. Exploring how other water filled things float and sink. Cartesian divers.
Sponges	Observation, what is it made from? Man-made and natural sponges. How much water does it absorb? Will it float or sink? How many holes are there and is there a pattern between holes and sinking/water absorbency?
Ice cube	How can you keep an ice cube in the classroom for the longest time? What could be designed? Create an ice-cube holder.

Table 1.1 *Creative practical activities*

Sand and yoghurt pots in a tray or sand tray	What proportion of sand and water do you need to make a good sandcastle?
Poppy seed heads	Seed dispersal. Thinking about what it might look like inside. What colour and size might the seeds be?
Seed packets: a variety of types need to be observed and discussed	Look at the picture of the plants on the seed packet. How big do pupils think the seed will be and why do they think this? What colour do they think they will be? Young children often think that tall plants will have big seeds and will be the same colour as the resulting plant. Opening the seed-packet is often very exciting for very young children and can lead to questions to test, whether the biggest seed produces the biggest plant. This can lead immediately to further investigation to extend children's experience of seed and plant beyond cress. (△ Ensure seeds are not treated with pesticides)
Hole-punch	How does it work? What does the spring do? Link to forces. Looking at other springs, e.g. pogo sticks. Helps children make connections.
Deflated balloon, ice balloon, water balloon, air balloon	Initial observation of the 4 balloons will lead to noticing differences and similarities between them. Pupils can be asked to describe each of the balloons and the vocabulary used noted. Younger children can have their observations scribed for them. What children notice about the balloons could lead to many questions. Pupils can be asked to raise questions. Questions raised can then be 'scanned' by the teacher for productive questions and these can lead to specific activities, e.g. What happened when they are put in water? Will each balloon bounce? How high will it bounce? How high will it bounce on different surfaces? What is the weight of the balloons? Here younger children can compare weights, older pupils can use instruments to measure.
Bubbles	Bubbles provide an excellent starting point for many observations. Vocabulary can be noted, observations can be shared and, if necessary, revisited. Different sizes and shapes of wands can be used to find out whether the shape of the wand affects the shape of the bubbles.

Tea bags	Looking at the similarities and differences between tea bags. Close examination of different bags under a hand lens and digital microscope to find out the size of the holes. Weighing the tea in different bags. Looking at the shape of the tea leaves under a digital microscope. Making tea at not more than 60 degrees Celsius. Looking at the colour of different teas. Which tea bag makes the strongest tea in five minutes?
Soap	Which soap washes paint off quickest? Warm and cold water can also be tested. How long before feet go wrinkly? Placing feet in warm water and seeing how long before they wrinkle. Drawing feet after. How much lather does a bar make? Testing different types of soap, turning the bar in hands once and then rubbing them together and comparing amounts of lather.

Creativity

Creativity is not just about the 'arts', although having creative development as part of the Foundation Stage explicitly related only to these subjects adds to the confusion. Creativity is not necessarily arriving at a new invention or a totally new idea. It can also be about approaching a familiar idea in a new way. Creativity is not absolute and should relate to the pupils' ages and previous experiences. A pupil who designs an innovative way to test out an idea is still being creative even if older learners have already published this method. It is also important to distinguish between a teacher who teaches in a creative way and a teacher who enables pupils to be creative in their approach. In fact, both are important. Some of the most creative teachers are so effective at performance that the pupils' role is only to sit and enjoy!

Ideas do not need to be novel or sophisticated to be approached in an interesting, creative way and most teachers can recount a great lesson, which was 'great' because of the creative outcome produced by the pupils. For example, when for homework some pupils were provided with an ice cube and challenged to find a way of keeping it from melting, the pupils were enabled to be creative. Although some pupils returned to school with only an ice cube, others created boxes, used a range of materials and devised elaborate holders. The most effective way found, on this occasion, to keep the ice cube from melting for the longest period of time, was by surrounding the ice cube with frozen peas in a plastic drinking cup. Having produced the winning design this pupil was still questioning whether the length of time the peas had been in the freezer would affect the time taken to melt. This example highlights that it is part of the teacher's role to seek out new ways of approaching old ideas to make them interesting and challenging to their pupils.

Summary

This chapter has considered a number of important points related to science, the nature of science and the approach of science in the primary curriculum. It has shown that science knowledge and understanding has to be provided for alongside the development of procedural understanding and process skills; that for the future well-being of the individual and society pupils' attitudes towards and in science must not be ignored.

There is a need to move away from the view that promotes science as a stuffy subject full of facts to be learned. This view needs to be replaced with an approach to teaching that envisions science and the teaching of science as a creative activity. If this is to be successful, then teachers need to give full consideration to pupils' ideas and to utilise these to further pupils' understanding of science in everyday life. The challenge for today's primary teacher is to break from the traditional mould and to teach science in a creative way making it more relevant to the future generation of 'could be' scientists.

CHAPTER 2

The Skills Pupils Need to Learn Science – Process Skills

Hellen Ward and Judith Roden

Introduction: The Scientific Process

This chapter will explore the process skills and their role in developing pupils' knowledge and understanding of science. It will identify and consider the importance of developing these skills evident in Sc1, Scientific Enquiry. Although termed the process skills, these skills are also thought of as the basic skills. These basic skills are embedded into Sc1 within the National Curriculum and, whilst sometimes implicit rather than explicit, they form the backbone of the curriculum. The main aim of this chapter is to look at ways in which teachers can structure the experiences provided so these skills are developed within the half-term science topic or scheme of work.

Developing Children's Process Skills

Initially, children's process skills are limited and unsystematic, and characterised by trial and error exploration. It is part of the teacher's role to help develop these so that, as they get older, pupils approach the exploration of the world in a more systematic, organised and meaningful way. Unconsciously, young children make use of simple individual process skills all the time during their exploration of the world but, as they get older, individual skills become more important in their formal education. The simpler skills involve observing, comparing, classifying and questioning but these are fundamental to the development of more advanced skills such as planning, predicting and data interpretation. It is not suggested that as pupils move through school that they need more opportunities to practise using process skills in total, but rather to focus specifically on one or more of the skills on particular occasions. In other words, it is important for teachers to identify individual process skills and to provide the opportunity for pupils to practise each skill that make up procedural understanding. This will enable improved application of individual skills and, over time, there should also be opportunities to link these skills enabling pupils to develop a more sophisticated use of the whole process. This implies that teachers need to identify individual process skills at the planning stage and to make these the focus of the learning intentions. This careful planning focusing on process skill intentions alongside those related to knowledge and understanding should, in time, allow for 'fine tuning' of the whole process.

The stages of investigating an idea are a useful starting point when identifying skills. See Figure 2.1.

---

1. Selection of the global question*
2. Identification of the independent variables
3. Thinking of how to measure/observe the outcome (dependent variable)
4. Question generation
5. Selecting the equipment and deciding how to use it
6. Deciding what might happen (making a prediction) if needed*
7. Data collection methods – type and amount of data to be collected*
8. Making observations and measurements
9. Recording and evaluating the data (reliability)
10. Interpreting the data
11. Drawing conclusions
12. Evaluating the process*

*Using secondary sources of information can occur at a number of points. It will differ according to the investigation as well as age of pupils, but is an important part of the process.

Figure 2.1 *Stages of scientific enquiry*

Within the National Curriculum: planning; obtaining and presenting evidence; and considering and evaluating evidence; are the elements of scientific enquiry, together with the nature of scientific ideas. Focusing first on the skills involved with planning investigative work, these are composed of:

■ questioning and question selection

■ variable/factor identification and selection

■ predicting

■ equipment selection

■ fair testing.

Level	Questioning	Prediction	Observation and measurement	Use of equipment	Use of texts	Data collection and recording	Variable selection (Fair test)	Communication of result	Evaluate	Data interpretation
Level 1			Describe or respond to simple features			Use drawings, simple charts		Communicating findings in simple ways		
Level 2	Respond to and, **with help**, make their own	Say whether what happened was what they expected	Make observations related to their task	Use simple equipment provided	Use simple texts, **with help**	Using simple tables		Describe observations using scientific vocabulary		
Level 3	Respond to suggestions and put forward own ideas		Make relevant observations and measure quantities, such as length or mass	Use a range of simple equipment	Use simple texts to find information	Variety of ways used (tables, diagrams, charts, Venn diagrams, bar graphs)	Carry out a fair test **with some help**, recognising and explaining why it is fair	Provide explanations for observations and measurements		Provide explanations for simple patterns
Level 4	**Decide** on an appropriate approach (questions raised by pupils but within framework provided)	Make predictions	Make a series of both, adequate for the task	Select suitable equipment	From sources provided for them	Tables and bar charts, bar and simple line graphs	Able to vary one factor while keeping others the same	Begin to relate conclusions to patterns and scientific K&U using appropriate scientific language	Suggest improvements giving reasons	Use graphs to point out and interpret patterns in data
Level 5	**Identify** an appropriate approach (questions and context identified by pupils)	Make predictions based on scientific K&U	Make a series of observations, comparisons or measurements with **precision**. Begin to **repeat** these	Select equipment for a range of tasks and plan to use it effectively	Select from a range of sources	Systematically and, where appropriate, present data as line graphs	Identify key factors to be considered	Conclusions that are consistent with the evidence and begin to relate to scientific K&U. Using appropriate scientific language	Practical suggestions about how their working methods could be improved	Offer simple explanations for any differences encountered. Use conventions to communicate quantitative and qualitative data

Table 2.1 *Process skills mapped against the level descriptions*

Obtaining and presenting evidence includes:

- making observations

- measuring using both standard and non standard units

- recording in a variety of ways

- using equipment with varying degrees of precision

- controlling hazards and risks.

Considering and evaluating evidence forms the final part of the process from a National Curriculum point of view. The skills associated with this aspect are:

- describing – identifying patterns and trends

- concluding – identifying where data supports any predictions made and where new ideas can be generated

- explaining – using scientific knowledge and understanding

- evaluating – identifying limitations and significance of findings and methods.

These skills have been identified in the National Curriculum Attainment Target 1 (level descriptions). These are presented in a developmental way in Table 2.1.

Questioning and Question-Raising

It is widely accepted that pupils bring previous knowledge to a new situation and this forms the basis upon which to extend their understanding. In order to extend their knowledge, pupils should be encouraged to ask questions about the world around them. Being asked to raise questions and to find their own answers enables pupils to relate new ideas to a previous experience and to draw upon their current knowledge and understanding. Pupils will, and do raise their own appropriate questions that can be investigated. Questioning, alongside observation and enquiry, is a key aspect of developing children's understanding of the world. Pupils need to understand the difference between the questions they ask that can be investigated, those that will be answered using other approaches and those that do not have an answer. Clearly, then, it is important to encourage pupils' questions and there are a variety of ways to do this.

The use of a 'question box' in the classroom helps involve the pupils in the learning process. Pupils post their questions about the unit of work under study and these questions are then selected by the teacher and focused upon on a weekly basis. This helps to show that the pupils' questions are important and valued, and links them effectively into classroom work. It is also a good idea to have a 'problem' corner or a 'question of the week' for pupils to pursue in their free time. Displays can include enquiry questions, and a question board is another strategy that encourages the involvement of pupils. The questions are shared in a visual way and pupils can then find the answers and add these to the wall display (Figure 2.2). The answers can come from work in lessons as well as self-study or homework activities.

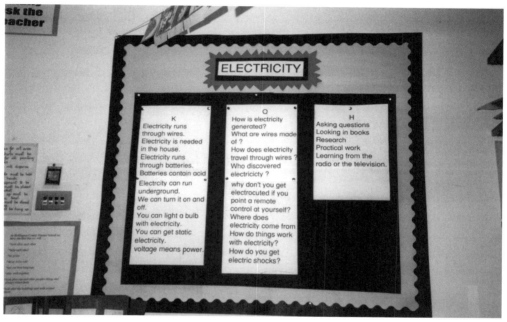

Figure 2.2 *Displaying pupils' questions and the answers found*

The KWHL grid (K = What I Know; W = What I want to know; H = How I will find out; L = What I have learned) also facilitates the raising of pupils' questions at the start of a unit of work. The items in the 'Know' column can be used to focus upon areas of misconception and the questions raised can encourage pupils' interest in lessons. Although not all of the questions will be asked in a form that can be investigated practically, many can be used as a starting point for appropriate practical work and others will be answered by using secondary sources.

Whilst pre-school children seem continually to ask questions, some older pupils seem to have lost this ability. This might be because traditional teaching has not required pupils to ask questions or, more often, pupils are not encouraged to ask questions because teachers have been afraid of not knowing the answers. In the recent climate pupils' questions have been somewhat irrelevant with the trend towards the widespread use of inflexible schemes of work that provide little opportunity for work to be tailored to meet the needs of individuals. Worryingly, a recent HMI report (2004) suggests that although teachers elicit pupils' original ideas, little action is taken to alter the work planned.

Enabling pupils to define their own questions is an important feature of investigative work and one that should take place initially in basic skills lessons, as pupils need to be taught how to ask investigative questions. It would be ideal if pupils could, following this starting point, go on to try out their ideas. However, time for science in the primary curriculum has become squeezed in recent years and therefore time to follow through all starting points to a complete investigation would not, in itself, enable the basic skill of questioning to be developed.

Global Questions

Teachers can help to scaffold pupils' learning in investigative work by providing a 'global question' as a starting point. This enables the pupils to begin to identify variables offering a way whereby pupils can generate appropriate questions within an investigative framework.

Using the global question 'How can we keep a drink hot for the longest time?' provides the opportunity to identify many variables. However, in a lesson where the focus is upon the skill of question-raising, it is important for the teacher to select the variables to be used, for example selecting the factor to change (independent variables) as 'the type of liquid' and the factor to measure (the dependent variable) as 'temperature over time'. From this starting point pupils can then identify specific questions and this process should be supported by modelling and shared writing. The questions that result could be 'What happens to the temperature of different liquids over time?' or 'What happens to the temperature of liquids over time?' or even 'Which liquid will cool the quickest?' Discussion, alteration and refinement of these questions can then occur, further developing the pupils' skills in question-raising.

As modelling allows pupils to develop their skills further than if they were unaided, the support should be reduced over time and the pupils should be provided with opportunities to practise their newly developed skill: pupils should be given the opportunity to generate new questions using the same global question but with different variables. For example, if instead of the type of liquid, the independent variable could be changed to 'the type of materials the cup is made out of', different questions will be formulated, e.g. 'Which material will kee drink hotter for longer?' or 'Which material is the most effective at keeping drink hot?' or 'What happens to the temperature of the liquid in different type: of cup?' Some pupils' questions will be more refined than others and discussion of this should be a teaching point. Eventually pupils will go on to identify the global question themselves.

Variable Identification and Selection

Although discussed as a separate skill from questioning, identification of variables and question development can be promoted from similar starting points. Variables are also called 'factors'. Those that can be changed are termed the independent variables, whilst those that can be observed and/or measured are called the dependent variables.

Brainstorming initially all independent variables for an investigation, using a global question is a good starting point. If using the global question 'How can we keep a drink hot until lunchtime?', with some prompting from the teacher the pupils should be able to identify what could be changed in order to keep the drink hot. In this example, the independent variables include the type of liquid, the amount of liquid, the size of cup, the type of cup, whether the cup is wrapped, if it has a lid or the number of lids. When given the opportunity, pupils do not usually find identifying variables difficult; in fact, they often enjoy the challenge.

Identifying the dependent variables is more problematic. These are the outcomes of the test, the temperature drop of the liquid or the time in the air of the spinner. Some pupils will identify with the term 'measurement' and will think of measuring the liquid. However, the amount of liquid is one of the variables that can be changed and measuring the amount of liquid will not lead to data that will answer their question 'which is the hottest?' Highlighting the different variables for changing and measuring using different coloured Post-it notes, one colour for those variables that can be changed and another colour for those that can be measured, helps the pupils to identify and recognise these different features (Figure 2.3).

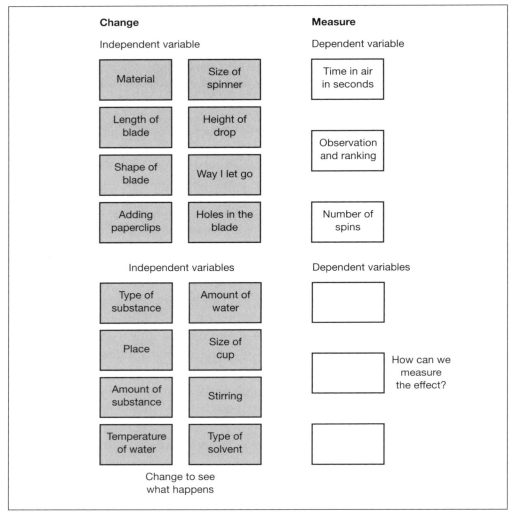

Figure 2.3 *Post-it notes and skills lessons for variable and question-raising skills lessons*

Predicting

The making of predictions is a common feature of most primary classrooms. In fact, this could be seen as one of the key outcomes of the National Curriculum's impact on practice at Key Stages 1 and 2. Prediction making, currently, is probably one of the few science skills focused upon in many infant and junior classrooms. Many lessons start with the question 'What do you think will happen?' before any equipment is used or any activity is undertaken. Whilst prediction is an important skill, perhaps this emphasis or overemphasis should be evaluated.

With very young pupils, asking for a prediction will often result in the response 'I don't know'. Using the ubiquitous 'cars down ramps' scenario, where pupils are asked which car will travel the furthest after being let go at the top of a ramp, often results in pupils selecting a car of a particular colour because it is their favourite. This is the 'I like blue, because blue is the best' response. Pupils, at this stage, do not have a well-defined or developed understanding of why things happen and yet they are frequently asked to make a prediction. The result of this emphasis is twofold. First, pupils are asked to make a prediction when their knowledge and understanding of the aspect are limited and, secondly, teachers pre-judge an outcome. When carrying out work with the cars, the pupils either find that their ideas are wrong, so they 'cheat' to ensure their prediction becomes correct, or they change their prediction to match the findings, understanding only that they were wrong. Sadly, the pupils unconsciously receive the inappropriate message that making a prediction is an element of science that 'proves' that science has the right answer and that perhaps their role is to find it.

Teachers often also expect that the outcomes of the work will 'prove' a fact. It is really important that pupils are allowed to carry out their own investigation, collect and interpret their own data and then consider what their data tells them, i.e. draw their own conclusions based on consideration of the collected evidence. It is tempting for teachers, anxious for their pupils to get the 'right answer', to suggest that some data are disregarded.

Case Study 2.1

One group of Year 6 children working on a topic of mini-beasts, carried out a simple practical task to find out where woodlice like to live. The pupils were asked to test different materials and to set up a survey. They were given a shoe-box with a lid and a range of materials from which to line sections of the box to find out if the woodlice had preferences. The pupils carried out their observational activities and recorded the time the woodlice spent in the different places by time sampling and tallying the numbers of individuals in each location. The results of all the groups were fed back to the teacher at the end of 30 minutes.

The result was that all but one of the groups demonstrated that the woodlice preferred the damp area. However, one group found that their woodlice spent more time in the straw. Although their findings did not concur with other groups, their results were consistent with the data collected by their observations. These unexpected results neither tallied with their own prediction, nor with that of their class teacher. Unfortunately, the teacher stated that their results were wrong and that they should not write their findings as their conclusion. Worryingly, they were required to write the conclusions obtained by the rest of the class.

Pre-judging an outcome is problematic because it promotes the idea that there is one answer and that the pupils' role is to hunt it out! This is not helpful to pupil learning and does not reflect the way in which scientists work. Professor Lewis Wolpert, one of the Acclaim scientists (www.acclaimscientists.org.uk), when asked what would he do if his experiment did not work stated, 'Try to understand why'. It is important here to note that science develops through things that do not work as much as through those that do and that this is true also of how children's understanding of science develops.

It is clear from Attainment Target 1 (Table 2.1) that making a prediction first appears at Level 4. This is the expectation for an average Year 6 pupil. At Level 2 the expectation is that pupils should be asked about their ideas after they have finished their work. Yet, in common practice, even young pupils are continually asked to give a reason for why things might happen in advance of it happening. Even adults when asked to give a prediction if they have no previous experience or knowledge to use are actually put off. In the same way, asking young pupils to make a prediction when they have little prior evidence to apply to the situation can be equally off-putting and threatening. Therefore teachers should refrain from formally requesting a prediction in every activity. This view does not, however, preclude the teacher from taking notice if pupils spontaneously provide suggestions about what they think might happen. This could be recorded on the pupil's work and reflected upon with them, at a later time. In fact, this would indicate good practice, not least in terms of differentiation.

Equipment Selection and Use

In the early years of primary education, pupils are expected to use equipment provided for them by their teacher and only later are they required to select their own. However, it is difficult for pupils to choose appropriate instruments to use if they have had limited experience of using relevant resources. Therefore, pupils need to be shown particular pieces of equipment and need to be taught explicitly how to use them. Whilst it is common practice in mathematics for time to be spent in teaching pupils how to use equipment using a range of approaches, sadly, in science, equipment is often introduced as part of an activity. Instead, scientific equipment should be introduced to the pupils and should be the focus of the learning intention. This then not only allows pupils to make an informed choice about which equipment to use in an activity, but will enable them to use the equipment correctly and make more accurate measurements.

Case Study 2.2

Using a Newton meter is a prime example of a resource that is often not introduced before it is used. When first introduced, many pupils are not often aware of forces in everyday life let alone aware of how they may be measured. Before the Newton meter or spring balance is introduced to pupils they need to have had opportunities to push objects with springs and to see the effects of this on the spring. Following this, they should go on to to pull and contract springs as part of simple work on forces. (Springs are not expensive pieces of equipment and bags of 500 springs suitable for this purpose can be brought very cheaply.) Pupils should then be introduced to a range of Newton meters and be asked to find similarities and differences between them (10N and 20N, or 10N and 5N). The teacher should then allow the pupils to explore using the Newton meters. Initially, teachers should model how to do this, as less equipment is broken when pupils are taught how to hold the meters correctly. The correct way to hold the Newton meter is to hold it at the top with one hand and to place a little finger of the other hand in the hook at the bottom. Pupils need to pull down on the hook gently using only this little finger. Then, the adult should ask questions to focus the pupils' attention. 'What happens to the spring when you pull down gently?' 'What happens to the spring when you stop pulling and allow the spring to return?' Changing over to different types of Newton meters enables pupils to obtain information in order to make generalisations. The bigger and thicker the spring, the harder it is to pull. Playing a guessing game in pairs helps pupils to gain an understanding of this measurement of force. Whilst one pupil places their little finger on the hook of the Newton meter and closes their eyes, the other pupil holds the top and asks the first pupil to pull a force a set number of Newton's, e.g. 4N. When the pupil pulling thinks they have pulled the requested amount of force, they open their eyes and check the scale. With pupils changing over roles and using different force meters they not only become very accurate in estimation and scale reading, but also gain a clearer idea of what a Newton feels like.

It is crucial that before pupils are asked to make and record measurements that they have been introduced to the relevant equipment in this way. Otherwise their results will not be accurate, and therefore not reliable, and the pupils will not be able to explain their findings.

Fair-testing

Pupils need some guidance when they are identifying the independent and the dependent variables. Although often identified as one of the process skills, fair-testing is actually a procedure of science. This procedure provides a platform to enable pupils to carry out the work in a scientific way, called the fair test. Whilst fair-testing is only one aspect of the scientific method, it is the aspect focused upon extensively in the primary science curriculum. This has led to many pupils and teachers seeing the 'fair test' as the only method of practical science and, often, most science activities are carried out using the fair test model. The method is confusing for young children because of the term 'fair' which to them means not to cheat. Scientifically a fair test is one where only one variable is changed and all the rest remain constant. It is the inability to keep all the factors constant that makes this method ineffective for some investigations. Plants, humans and other animals are living things with genetic differences. These differences can play havoc with the result unless large enough samples are used. These other factors, the hidden ones, also affect results. A good example of a hidden factor can be demonstrated using the simple plants experiment.

Case Study 2.3

In a typical lesson on plants the factors that affect growth are selected. The teacher and pupils talk about what to test, and decide upon altering the amount of light keeping the amount of water, soil, type of plant, etc. the same. The outcome is to be measured by comparing the height or colour of the leaves. One plant is placed on the windowsill, one in a cupboard and another under a table, and a fair test is started. However, the plant on the windowsill does not grow as expected. This plant experiences the greatest range of temperatures, as it is in the hottest place in the day and the coldest place at night, sometimes by as much as 20 °C. This temperature change is a hidden factor which can cause the plant, and the teacher, stress. Another hidden factor is the genetic make-up of the plant. Both will impact upon the results and make it difficult to 'prove' the point being illustrated. A survey using more plants and obtaining a greater range of information would have been scientifically more accurate or 'fair'.

Extending the types of investigations that the pupils are exposed to is essential. Going back to watching and recording change over time, surveying, problem-solving and observations are vital. By planting a number of bean plants at the rate of one a day for two weeks, and monitoring their growth, the practical skills developed as a result are far greater than those which would have been obtained from watching one seed germinate. This is not an investigation but an observational task – a valid science activity – and will provide the pupils with opportunities to learn about science and then use these skills to carry out their own investigations. However, in order for this to take place, more value and status must be given to non-fair test activities and a greater understanding of methods of science is needed. In the 1800s 300 stones fell from the sky near a village in France called Laigle. Before the stones landed there were bright lights in the sky and craters were made in the ground. Using data collected from observations, scientists decided that the rocks had come from space. This deduction had no fair test element or planning attached to it, however, it was still effective science. The scientists obviously did not plan this event, but the method of gaining understanding about the world was still a valid one. Observations can be planned, and an immense amount of planning and testing occurred prior to the invention of the first microscope. Valuing other aspects of science, in addition to the fair test, is vital if progress is to be made in developing creative-thinking individuals for the future.

Checking Observation and Data

Once observations and measurements have been made it is important that pupils critique these. Taking more than one reading in a practical investigation is expected from the end of Key Stage 1, although the expectation is that 7-year-olds will add the totals or take the middle number. At this stage looking at the readings and checking for odd results must be simply taught. Checking readings allows the reliability of the readings to be gauged. Pupils can be taught to identify unusual results and to repeat these. This skill should be taught in basic skills lessons and then should be practised during complete investigations.

Using a Range of Recording Strategies

Currently, creativity in science is being stifled by the use of a limited number of methodologies and outdated recording strategies. Pupils are often expected to record using the traditional method, the 'apparatus, result and conclusion' approach for every piece of work. Whilst practice in literacy has developed over the last five years with the introduction of skill-based lessons, this has not happened in science teaching. There is no primary science strategy to guide teachers towards alternative recording methods and for many teachers their only experience of science has been gained from their own secondary school education. Rather than pupils being required to record what they have done and their findings in a more imaginative way, an outdated method of recording is disadvantaging both the less literate and more literate alike. The method of recording adopted is often as a result of requiring evidence of work completed to be in the pupils' books. Worse still, the work is often written on the board by

the teacher for pupils to copy. Whilst the modelling and support that are sometimes provided in this shared writing element are recommended, the copying of
the shared text by all pupils is as unacceptable in science as it would be in literacy, because it is just handwriting practice.

This practice does little to fire the imagination of young impressionable
pupils as their attitudes towards science are being formed. An HMI report suggested that many pupils could not even read the work that they had written in
their books. Instead, pupils should be encouraged to use pictures, drawings and
diagrams as well as cartoon strips, poems and posters to record their work in
science (see, for example, Figure 2.4).

To have the greatest impact, recording should occur throughout the lesson,
not just at the end. Pupils need to be introduced to the different ways of recording in the same way as they need to be introduced to resources. Teachers need
to select a different method of recording to model, and where possible should
be the focus of the learning intention. This then enables a range of recording
opportunities to be provided throughout the year so that at a later stage, when
pupils are asked to choose their own, most appropriate method, they have a
repertoire from which to select.

The use of word banks and individual pupil science dictionaries promotes
pupil independence. Recording in science also requires mathematical skills of
drawing tables and graphs. Modelling and breaking these activities down into
small steps helps pupils to develop their recording skills.

Identifying Patterns, Trends in Data and Data Interpretation

Pupils need to be taught how to present data, e.g. drawing diagrams and
graphs, as well as having the opportunity to interpret these. Interpreting data
relies heavily on seeing patterns or relationships between things that can be
observed. This skill is closely linked with the skill of evaluating. Specific lessons
need to be planned across the key stage where time is devoted to this skill,
enabling pupils to find the patterns and draw inferences for themselves. An
important part of pattern-seeking is being able to describe what is seen. Pupils
therefore need the support of the teacher to develop the appropriate vocabulary
and to know what to identify. Pattern-seeking is about describing what is seen
rather than explaining why it happens. Providing graphs and asking questions
related to these enable pupils to learn how to interpret the graphs. This is initially difficult for many pupils as graphing skills usually focus upon the drawing
of the minutiae rather than the broad patterns within.

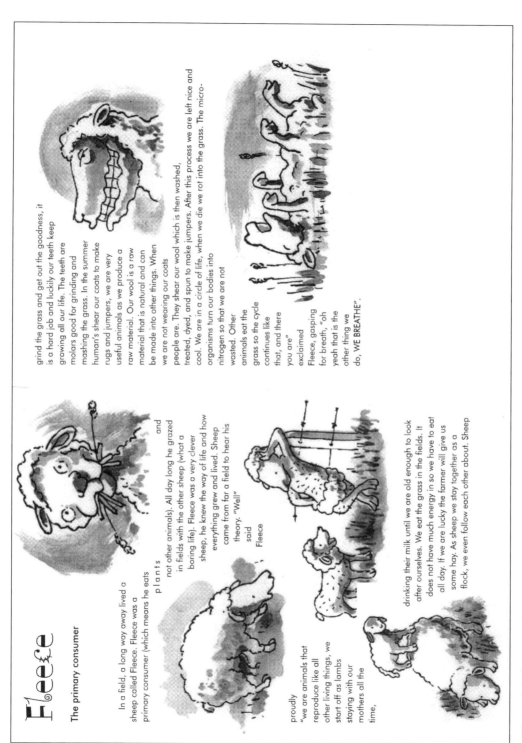

Figure 2.4 *A range of recording strategies can be seen on the website:* *www.paulchapmanpublishing.co.uk\resources\ward.pdf* *Fleece is a story by a Year 6 child.*

Rarely would identifying the patterns and trends take up a complete science lesson, so after identifying the patterns and trends the pupils can then try out one of the tasks. As pupils often have difficulties in interpreting patterns and trends, starting a lesson in this way is helpful. Frequently, insufficient time is devoted to this aspect of learning in science as these are often left to the end of an illustrative or investigative activity. Consequently, for many pupils, their ability to identify patterns, to see trends in data and to interpret what their data tell them are often underdeveloped. In other words, pupils are not being provided with sufficient opportunity to develop the higher order skills in science as carrying out the activity and recording the result are viewed as more important.

Drawing Graphs

Drawing graphs is hard! The process of graph-drawing requires spatial awareness and teachers need to provide pupils with support for graph-making. A good introduction is to start with examples of graphs that have mistakes on them, as asking pupils to 'spot the deliberate mistakes' helps them to identify what features a graph should contain. Teaching pupils graph-drawing skills and allowing opportunities to practise this skill does work. Pupils can become very good at drawing graphs, and this can be related directly to detailed teaching.

Conclusions

Drawing conclusions makes pupils aware of what they have found and why it is relevant, but few pupils find this easy. Concluding is a crucial, basic skill that is made easier if pupils have developed enough appropriate scientific vocabulary. Providing opportunities for pupils to evaluate conclusions written by others supports this process and helps pupils to identify what are the features of a good explanation and how they differ from descriptions. Providing skill lessons that focus upon a set of prewritten conclusions with modelling and scaffolding by the teacher is vital. Pupils should not write down the statements or conclusions that have been modelled with them, but should always try to improve or alter the ones that have been discussed. This process also supports scientific understanding and the content of the statements can be altered in order to target the skill of drawing appropriate conclusions based on evidence.

Evaluating Ideas

The evaluation of the way in which an activity proceeded is required, as is questioning the reliability of the data collected. Evaluation is important because pupils need to review, critically, the methods used in order to make suggestions for future work. Furthermore, pupils also need to discuss what they have done and why, and to think about how else they might have completed the task or recorded the information. When teachers allow this to happen, they allow pupils to actively evaluate their own learning. Providing a structure for this to happen such as a series of questions scaffolds the process. Where pupils are not supported in this process they evaluate the work in a non-scientific way. In one case a group of 10-year-olds were asked to evaluate the work: 'it would have been better if Kirsty had not been sick in the bucket' was the response. A group of infants, who were not used to investigating or evaluating their work suggested 'it was fun, do not change it at all'.

Summary

The importance of the process skills that are needed in order to undertake scientific enquiry has been highlighted throughout this chapter. The chapter has shown the need for teachers to plan directly for and to include activities in science that will enable pupils to develop their science process skills progressively and systematically throughout their time in school thus developing procedural understanding. The chapters that follow will consider these issues in more depth; for example, the next chapter will focus more specifically on the skill of observation. Chapter 5 will take these skills and show how they are linked in investigating an idea.

CHAPTER 3

Observation, Measurement and Classification

Judith Roden

Introduction

This chapter will explore why it is important for children to be regularly provided with activities to develop their observation, measurement and classification skills, and also to provide suggestions for a range of activities that will help teachers to plan worthwhile activities for systematic study. Additionally, it will provide an explanation of how these can contribute to children's learning in science.

Observation in the Foundation Stage and National Curriculum

Observation, measurement and classification are fundamental aspects of both the Foundation Stage curriculum and within the Scientific Enquiry Strand (Sc1) of the National Curriculum at Key Stages 1 and 2. In order to develop children's knowledge and understanding of the world at the Foundation Stage, practitioners are required to give particular attention to activities based on first-hand exploration including observation (QCA, 2000, p.830). The Science National Curriculum (DfEE, 1999, p.16) requires pupils at Key Stage 1 to be taught that it is important to collect evidence by making observations and measurements when trying to answer a question, and at Key Stage 2 (DfEE, 1999, p.21) that it is important to test ideas using evidence from observation and measurement.

One point of note here is that the development of the process skills of observation, measurement and classification, asking questions, etc. should not be taught separately, but should be set in the context of other National Curriculum

Programmes of Study. This means that teachers should focus learning intentions on observation, measurement and classification, and they should regularly provide specific tasks that require pupils to make observations and measurements in relation to living things, materials and their properties and physical processes.

It is crucial that children are provided with opportunities to observe the finer detail of things across Sc2, Sc3 and Sc4, and that this should be included in schemes of work across the whole of the 3–11-year age range. This not only helps to interrelate Sc1 into the other programmes of study, but also should enable children to build up an understanding of things systematically across the various aspects of science. For example, when looking at aspects of Sc2, pupils could observe things from the natural living world, e.g. small creatures, leaves or flowers, etc. By doing so, pupils will also develop their understanding of, for example, the diversity of living things, the parts of a flower or parts of a leaf. Observation and drawing of a number of different kinds of pine cones (or rocks or shells or leaves) will reveal the differences there are between things which are similar. In the same way, in relation to Sc3, pupils could look closely at a variety of fabrics, or paper or wood or stone which could lead to simple investigations to find out, for example, which fabric absorbs the most water, or which is the best wrapping paper with which to wrap up Christmas parcels, or which is the best paper for writing on. When the focus of study is on Sc3, pupils might be encouraged to note the finer parts of unconnected small light bulbs. Here, noting similarities and differences between bulbs of different voltages may well lead directly to questions about the size of filaments and simple investigations to find out what happens when the different bulbs are connected, one by one, into the same simple electrical circuits.

Observational drawings provide excellent opportunities for pupils to record their observations and measurements. Here, teacher questions should focus on pupils looking for detail and patterns etc. Some might argue that observational drawing is more of an art than a science activity, however, in science it is different because the learning intentions are different. The learning intention in science is not about the quality of the drawing, but more about recording observed features, noticing detail and patterns, and identifying similarities and differences etc.

The use of frames or 'peepholes' can focus on the detail of a small area rather than on gross external features. Use of peepholes provides a less threatening situation than asking pupils to draw a whole object as only one small part has to be focused on. This is an excellent activity for encouraging pupils to focus on detail. It is important to realise that it is legitimate, and important, to have process skills learning intentions in addition to those relating to knowledge and understanding, or sometimes exclusively. So it is important to indicate this explicitly in long-, medium- and short-term plans as well as in lesson plans. It is important to remember that here the focus is on developing the process skills.

Level	AT1: Scientific Enquiry	AT2: Life Processes and Living Things	AT3: Materials and their Properties	AT4: Physical Processes
Foundation Stage	Describe simple features of objects. Investigate objects and materials by using all their senses as appropriate.	Examine living things to find out more about them. Find out about and identify some features of living things they observe. Observe, find out about and identify features in the place they live and the natural world.	Show curiosity, observe and manipulate objects. Describe simple features of objects and events.	Examine objects to find out more about them. Find out about and identify some features of objects and events they observe.
Level 1	Pupils describe or respond appropriately to simple features of objects, living things and events they observe.	Pupils communicate observations of a range of animals and plants ... in terms of features [for example colour of coat, size of leaf]. They recognise and identify a range of common animals; fly, goldfish, robin.	Pupils know about a range of properties, e.g. texture, appearance and communicate observations of materials in terms of these properties.	Pupils communicate observations of changes in light, sound or movement that results from actions, e.g. switching on a simple electrical current, pushing or pulling objects. They recognise that sound and light come from a variety of sources and name some of these.
Level 2	Pupils use simple equipment provided and make observations related to their task. They observe and compare objects, living things and events. They describe their observations using scientific vocabulary and record them using simple tables when appropriate.	Pupils sort living things into groups using simple features. They describe the basis for their groups [e.g. number of legs, shape of leaf].	Pupils identify a range of common materials and know about some of their properties. They describe similarities and differences between materials. They sort materials into groups and describe the basis for their groupings in everyday terms [for example shininess, hardness, smoothness]. They describe the ways	Pupils ... recognise and describe similarities and differences related to a range of physical phenomena. They compare the way in which devices, for example, bulbs, work in different electrical circuits. They compare the brightness or colour of lights and the loudness or pitch of sounds. They compare the movement of different objects in terms of speed or direction.

(continued)

Table 3.1 *Progression in observation and measurement*

Level 3	in which some materials are changed by heating or cooling or by processes such as bending and stretching.	Pupils use their knowledge and understanding of materials when they describe a variety of ways of sorting into groups according to their properties	Pupils identify ways in which an animal is suited to its environment, e.g. a fish having fins to help it swim.	Pupils make relevant observations and measure quantities such as length or mass, using a range of simple equipment. They provide explanations for observations and for simple patterns in recorded measurements.
Level 4	Pupils describe and explain physical phenomena [... How the apparent position of the sun changes over the course of a day].	Pupils describe the differences between the properties of different materials.	Pupils use keys based on observable external features to help them to identify and group living things systematically.	Pupils select suitable equipment and make a series of observations and measurements that are adequate for the task. They record their observations, comparisons and measurements using tables and bar charts.
Level 5	Pupils use previous ideas to describe abstract ideas.	Pupils describe some metallic properties and use these properties to distinguish metals from other solids.	Pupils recognise that there is a great variety of living things and understand the importance of classification.	Pupils make a series of observations, comparisons or measurements with precision appropriate to the task. They begin to repeat observations and measurements and to offer simple explanations for any differences they encounter.

Table 3.1 *Continued*

As can be seen from Table 3.1, there is a progression in what is expected from pupils in terms of observation, measurement and classification as they progress from the Foundation Stage to Level 5 of the National Curriculum. Consequently, whilst activities provided for pupils may be similar in nature at the different levels, teachers need to place different expectations on different individuals and groups of pupils to ensure challenge and linear progression in learning.

Why Children should be Taught to Observe

Clearly, observation is important. Observation is a fundamental aspect of the learning process and, although the skill is taken much for granted in everyday life, it is crucial for making sense of the world from an early age. Without this first-hand experience, children may not question what is observed in their world. Observation provides the opportunity for children to explore the nature of objects and the relationship between objects. Observation, and more importantly, as they get older, critical observation promotes scientific thinking and contributes to children's understanding of science. Furthermore, initial observations can lead to the formulation of questions, hypotheses, predictions and conclusions.

Observation is also one of the most important process skills for developing knowledge of the natural and physical world. Here observation provides a good starting point for further exploration and investigation. It is widely accepted that children and adults learn about the world by using all their senses – touch, sight, smell, taste and hearing – and so children should regularly, when appropriate and with care, be asked to undertake activities specifically planned to develop the skill. Observation is therefore an important process skill, because it develops the ability to use all the senses appropriately and safely. Using all the senses, when appropriate, enables pupils to find patterns and develops the ability to sort and classify.

The role of the teacher in helping pupils to observe is crucial here as what teachers ask pupils to look for can have a significant effect on what is observed. Additionally, what children see is influenced by what they already know. Therefore, focused observation not only helps children to identify differences and similarities between objects or situations, but also helps them to see previously unnoticed patterns and to provide questions to be investigated further.

It is generally recognised that children find it more difficult to notice similarities because differences are often more obvious. Children also need to be encouraged to look for patterns and sequences in a series of observations especially in illustrative activities and investigations.

Ultimately, systematic observation, especially when collecting data, for example when measuring the temperature of water as it cools, leads children to become more able to make accurate observations.

Developing the skill of observation is important not only for the individual, but also for the wider development of scientific knowledge and understanding within the larger scientific community. In the past, great leaps in the development of scientific ideas, have come about from an initial starting point where noticing a small, possibly unusual, observation has led to a search for a new explanation to explain the observations or inconsistencies. This helps to explain how revolutions in scientific thinking have come about: for example, Newton's observation of the apple falling from a tree, Archimedes' observations of water levels or Priestley's exploration of what happens when something burns.

What Sort of Activities can Help Children to Develop their Observation Skills?

There are many basic observation activities that can be used across the age range. For example, at the earliest stages of education, observation enables pupils to gain information about a wide variety of different everyday objects. Children should regularly be asked to describe, e.g. a leaf, an apple, a book or a table fork. Thus enabling them to see similarities and differences between things that are very different. Building on this foundation, older children can be asked to describe objects that are very similar, e.g., to describe a number of different leaves, pine cones, seashells, rocks, etc. This leads to the recognition of characteristics by which scientists group things together. Older children need to be challenged to observe finer detail. This can be made more challenging by asking more able and older children for measurements to be included in the description.

A good activity for making children look more closely at objects makes use of a digital camera. Providing children with close-up photographs of an object and then asking them to identify the object from the picture is a good way to encourage fine observation. If pupils cannot identify the object immediately they can be challenged to 'go find the object'. This is a fun way to improve finer observational skills and children enjoy the experience. Younger children can be provided with photographs that may well seem obvious to older children and adults, for example see Figure 3.1.

Figure 3.1 *Close-up photograph of broccoli*

Pupils can be given a range of close-up photographs and the real objects can be placed around the room. Pupils are challenged to match the photo with the real object and asked to identify the object. Older children will enjoy a more difficult close-up photograph acting as detectives to find the answer (see, for example, Figure 3.2). Other examples are provided on the website: www.paulchapman-publishing.co.uk\resources\ward.pdf

Observational activities provide lots of scope for exploration and questioning. Children enjoy a challenge and 'mystery parcels' offers the opportunity to develop observation using a variety of senses and the development of vocabulary. For example an object can be wrapped in newspaper – a little like the children's party game 'pass the parcel'. Once it is wrapped, children can be asked to feel the parcel and to note any words used to describe it. After a short time they can be asked to try to identify the object from their observations, then to unwrap the object and note down further words to describe the object. Alternatively, an object could be placed in a shoebox, or smaller items, e.g. paperclips, a magnet, a piece of plasticene, could be placed in a matchbox.

Observational skills can also be developed through the use of simple games. The use of 'feely bags' are popular in many classrooms. Variations on the theme of 'Kim's' game provide children with the opportunity to look at a tray full of objects (fewer for younger children, more for older children) for a few minutes,

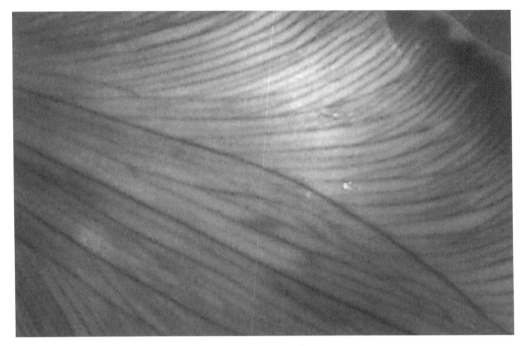

Figure 3.2 *Close-up photograph of a flower petal*

before having to recall what is on the tray. This game not only develops memory, but can be extended to differentiate not only what the object is, but also children can be asked to recall finer details like what colour the object is, how many wheels it has, finer details about the wheel, and for example, how many spokes it has. A tray of objects including a range of different objects made of different materials, e.g. balloon, plastic spoon, fabric and rubber ball. Children can play the 'yes/no' game where one child secretly chooses one item from the tray and others ask questions to try to identify the object. This will require pupils to think about the detail of an object and/or what it is made of. Some variations might include hard/soft, shiny/dull, natural/human-made. From a planning perspective, differentiation is 'built in' and is achieved by outcome.

Sorting and Classifying

Being asked to sort and classify provided objects naturally leads to seeing similarities and differences between objects (Figure 3.3). Sorting and classifying is also fundamental to science. Children need to be given many opportunities, starting from observation using all their senses, and from their earliest days in school, to develop systematically the skills of sorting and classifying. At the Foundation Stage and Key Stage 1, this mainly involves sorting based on gross features. Can pupils sort into 2 groups, 3 groups or 4 groups? A variation on this theme could be that the teacher sorts a group of objects and challenges the pupils to state which criterion has been used to classify. A further development could be where the teacher provides objects sorted into two groups and provides other objects for pupils to add to one of the groups. Pupils then need to explain why the new object belongs in the chosen group.

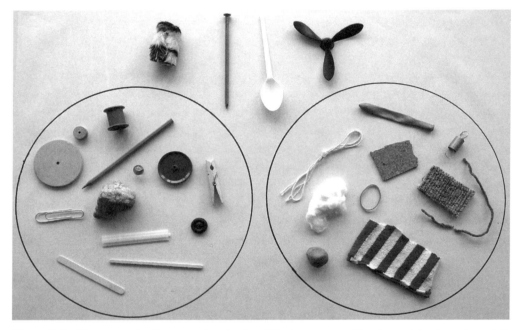

Figure 3.3 *Photograph of grouped objects. Which group do the four objects belong in?*

Children group from an early age, but are not able to give reasons for doing so. Children say that things just 'go together' instead of having the same characteristic. It is tempting to think that older children need not practise these basic skills, but they too need opportunities to notice more detail and to look for more sophisticated patterns within and between objects. Therefore at Key Stage 2, children should be challenged to make finer observations of everyday and more unusual objects.

Basic sorting not only leads to classification but in itself, helps to develop children's observation skills by asking them to examine detail to find out which groups they belong to. Observation in this context leads pupils to notice patterns, e.g. that all seashells have similarities and are made of the same material, but that differences between shells are often substantial. Finer observation of detail may reveal differences between other things that are basically 'the same', e.g. rocks, or a natural seasonal change like the discolouration of leaves in the autumn.

Children's Observations

Experience suggests that observations are frequently influenced by past experiences and therefore children's observations are often not what might be expected. Children will often observe what they think they can see, but actually it is often what is stored in their memory. Such observations are frequently 'contaminated' by their previous experience. For some pupils, observation is important because they may be being asked to look closely at some objects for the first time. Young children can often surprise adults by what they notice and it is important that their observations are not dismissed as being irrelevant. Young children make sense of things based on previous experience and therefore it should not be surprising when they appear to make what adults might think are irrelevant observations. In some ways young children's observations can be very limited whilst often being influenced by other things in their real world, like storybooks and other aspects of popular culture like videos and cartoons. Johnson (1996, p.32) says children's creative approach to observation needs to be encouraged and she says that children's drawings often show children's 'observation skills and creativity' and that these 'creative additions' indicate wider powers of observation. Furthermore, the way in which this manifests itself in children's drawings often differs according to gender. Girls tend to include more 'touchy feely' additions whilst boys generally will be more imaginative in their additions. However, there is an obvious tension here because on the one hand we want to encourage children to be creative, but on the other we want them to make accurate observations of things in their environment.

What Do Children Notice?

The three observational drawings of fish shown in Figure 3.4 are all drawings of the same trout drawn on the same day by Year 2/3 children. The fish was placed on a white tray in the middle of a large table and children were placed around the table and asked to draw the fish. The quality of the drawings varies enormously; fish 1 shows much immaturity in both observational and drawing skills, but indicates features observed by the child and reproduced on the drawing. Fish 2 has a noticeable head feature that is more reminiscent of a turtle, rather than a fish. Many people assessing fish 3 choose this as the best drawing of a fish, which it is, however, the drawing is typical of one that draws more from memory of pictures of fish than from observation of the fish on the table. The role of the teacher here is very important, as children need to be asked regularly what is being noticed to enable them to discriminate fine detail.

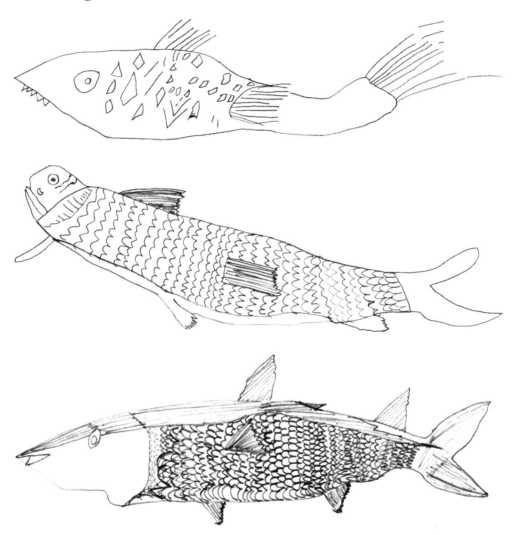

Figure 3.4 *Fish drawings. Other fish drawings are included on the website: www.paulchapmanpublishing.co.uk\resources\ward.pdf*

On the other hand, the drawings of various small creatures, drawn by Foundation Stage children, indicate that they have been influenced by remembered images of the creatures from books of fiction or other aspects of popular culture. In particular, it is noticeable that both the drawings of ladybirds have faces drawn on them (Figure 3.5). A crane-fly, whilst showing some very good observed features, provided a more creative impression rather than the observed creature. The crane fly, drawn by a boy had almost fairy-like qualities and the ladybirds, drawn by girls, have been given human-like characteristics. These are typical of young children's drawing of real things in their environment. The crane fly and other examples can be viewed on the website: www.paulchapmanpublishing.co.uk\resources\ward.pdf

Figure 3.5 *Drawings of ladybirds showing human-like characteristics*

Clearly, from a science point of view, whilst we would want to encourage creativity, we would prefer that the drawings here would focus on observable features and not include fanciful features perhaps influenced by children's literature and other media. One further problem here is that teachers will regularly praise highly such drawings based on their artistic, creative content rather than close observations.

Other activities that do not require such intense teacher input, within the context of life processes and living things, could include children sorting picture cards or model animals into groups. This leads directly on to classification of living things. Younger children will sort things familiar to themselves in various categories, for example whether they fly, walk or swim; alternatively they may group the 'scary' animals and the 'friendly' animals. Older children should be more able to group animals into scientific groups and, if not, should be challenged to do so. An activity like this can assess the extent to which pupils understand, for example, the vertebrate groups. Experience tells us that many adults as well as children will group amphibians (frogs, toads, salamanders and newts) with reptiles (lizards, snakes, etc). Whilst both groups have some similar features, there are major differences which need to be identified. Talking to children and students in training it is clear that they become more, not less, confused about animal groups as they get older. This needs to be dealt with at a simple level at the primary stage.

There are a number of misconceptions relating to animal groups that are commonly held by children and many adults. For example, young children will often be confused because although it can fly, a bat is a mammal. Similarly, a penguin can be confusing because although it is a bird, it does not fly. Dolphins are often considered to be fish rather than mammals, and the difference between reptiles and amphibians is not often clear. Whilst amphibians are those creatures that have a soft damp body and start their lives in water, reptiles tend to have scaly skins. Whilst frogs, toad, newts and salamanders are amphibians, lizards, snakes, turtles, crocodiles and alligators are reptiles. The confusion comes because newts and salamanders look like some lizards and many reptiles are amphibious, that is spend time in water and on land. Many adults are not clear about the difference between vertebrates, those animals with backbones, and invertebrates, those without backbones. In particular, worms, snakes and some lizards, e.g. slow-worms, are confused because at first glance they have similar features. Where invertebrates are concerned, many individuals have problems in relation to 'insects' where in everyday usage this often means all small creatures such as spiders, millipedes, etc., whereas the term insect, in science, relates specifically only to those creatures that have six legs, a thorax, a head and an abdomen.

Using models that are not made to scale, common in many Early Years' classrooms, also might lead to misconceptions with younger children. It also needs to be borne in mind that sometimes even identification books can help to promote misconceptions. Teachers and parents need to be aware of the possibility that identification books, e.g. entitled 'Insects', may well include animals for other subgroups, for example spiders, molluscs and crustaceans.

Making and Using Keys

Basic sorting leads to classification. The National Curriculum at both Key Stage 1 and Key Stage 2 requires children to use keys, but even Foundation Stage children can be introduced to simple keys made up by their teacher. Using keys can help pupils to become less confused about animal groups. This is one good reason for including them in teaching in the primary classroom. Use of keys should start off simply based on a very few different objects with very different characteristics. Older children need to be introduced progressively to more complex keys. Pupils at Key Stage 2 can be expected to be able to make keys. Once again, pupils should be introduced to this by being given fewer and very different objects and then asked to draw up a list of characteristics for each object. They can then be asked to make up a simple branching key. Coins could provide a good starting point for this. Once made, pupils could swap keys to see if they work.

Other Aspects of Observation

It is important to remember that observation in science includes all the senses and therefore it is appropriate for children to be asked to identify things using other senses. Children could undertake a 'senses survey' where they are asked to notice things deliberately placed in the room, e.g. a fan blowing at foot level; did they notice? A smell in the room, e.g. perfume or sliced onions revealed at a certain point in a session. Things to feel when blindfold, e.g. a teddy bear or rough sandpaper. Things to listen to, e.g. at what level of loudness can children first identify a tune well known to them? Can they identify taped noises, e.g. a tap running, a clock ticking, etc.?

Forms of Recording and Assessing Children's Observations

It is very tempting within the busy day of the classroom, to plan around activities that can produce a finished product for assessment purposes, e.g. a picture or a piece of writing. However, talk, what children say, is also an important form of evidence of pupil's ability to observe and should be recorded. An audio tape recorder can be useful here. As shown earlier, children's drawings are a very good way of recording observations. They may well provide the teacher with information about a child's understanding of scale and space, as well as how various parts fit together. For example, a child's drawing of the body might lead to an understanding of the way it works.

Summary

Observing is the skill of absorbing all information about the things around us. Children need to be encouraged to notice fine detail and go beyond what they expect to see. Children should develop the ability to distinguish what is relevant and what is not. They should be given the opportunity to record observations in a variety of ways including talk, writing or through their drawings.

The teacher's role in developing observation skills is not to be the fount of all knowledge. Rather, the teacher should enable children to see with 'new' eyes. They can do this by carefully structuring opportunities for the development of observation skills. Plenty of resources need to be provided; materials need to be selected carefully. Children need the opportunity to share their observations with others and need to be questioned about what they are noticing.

CHAPTER 4

Raising and Analysing Questions and Use of Secondary Sources

Judith Roden

Introduction

Chapter 3 explained how observation, as a fundamental skill, could lead pupils naturally to seeing patterns and sorting into groups leading to classification. Following on directly from Chapter 3, this chapter will focus more particularly on asking questions, which, along with measurement and classification, are often neglected skills within scientific enquiry. The nature of pupils' questions and how teachers can provide a role model will be explored. The chapter will also provide an analysis of teacher and pupil questions that form the basis for productive learning at an appropriate level in the primary classroom with examples of the questions that pupils ask and how these can be responded to.

Pupils Raising Questions within Statutory Requirements

Building on pre-school learning, in the Foundation Stage, there is an expectation that pupils will ask questions about why things happen and how things work (QCA, 2000, pp.88–9). Pupils are also expected to 'learn to investigate, be curious … pose questions, and use reference skills' (ibid.). Pupils should also be encouraged to suggest solutions to, and answers for, their own questions. Here the role of the teacher is crucial in providing a good role model when interacting with pupils playing with and exploring materials. This is particularly important when pupils are exploring materials at first hand in order to place them into simple groups as a precursor to classification.

During the primary years questioning forms part of the 'planning' at both key stages. At Key Stage 1 'pupils should be taught to ask questions (for example, 'How', 'Why', 'What will happen if … '? (DfEE, 1999, p.16) and decide how they might find answers to them. They should also 'use first-hand experience and simple information sources to answer questions' (ibid.). At Key Stage 2, naturally, the requirement is more demanding as pupils are expected to 'ask questions that can be investigated scientifically and decide how to find answers [and to] consider what sources of information, including first-hand experience and a range of other sources, they will use to answer questions' (DfEE, 1999, p.21).

Whilst in the Foundation Stage pupils will need help to find the answers to questions, by Key Stage 1 pupils should be encouraged to try to find their own answers, unaided, using a variety of books and Internet sources as well as being guided by the teacher to try to find answers to some questions by hands-on practical work. The role of the teacher here is to listen to pupils' ideas and to modify and develop them into something that can be investigated. Building on this, Key Stage 2 pupils should be able to access a wider range of sources to find answers to their 'why' questions and should be regularly challenged to discuss whether or not their questions can be answered by practical investigation rather than merely the use of secondary sources.

Traditionally, some teachers have viewed pupils' questions about science as a threat both to their authority and to their own knowledge and understanding, rather than as an aspect of learning to be encouraged. Whilst there is more understanding now, it is still true that some teachers are afraid of their pupils' questions on a subject they still feel less confident about. Frequently this has been borne out of teachers' perceptions that they should be able to answer all the questions asked of them, reflecting a now misguided view of the teacher as the 'fount of all knowledge'. This has led, perhaps unconsciously, to questioning being discouraged, although realistically, given the vastness of science, most teachers and even the most eminent of scientists cannot be expected to hold the answers to all the questions pupils might ask.

Although there is an expectation for teachers to focus on pupils' questions and to help pupils to develop their ability to raise questions, in practice this rarely happens. Teachers often argue that pupils do not ask questions and those that do ask questions teachers state that they find difficulty in knowing how to deal with. This is in part due to the unsophisticated way in which the questions are expressed and partly because many questions are difficult to answer directly. However, this is not a good enough reason to avoid questioning because, when pupils are given the opportunity to explore and investigate, questions are often an important by-product.

Providing a good role model here is crucial. Pupils of any age will not ask questions if they are not encouraged to look closely at things or to ask questions about them. Neither will they make progress in the types of questions to ask if the adults around them do not ask the kinds of questions that can lead to higher order thinking skills. 'Wait time' in science teaching is still an area that could be developed further, with the time between asking the question and expecting an answer still painfully inadequate. When pupils are given more time and the original question is not reworded or moved on to the next pupil, pupils have to begin to think for themselves and often astound teachers with their understanding.

Extending the type and function of questions is also needed. *Application questions*, i.e. those where the pupils have to think about the knowledge in a new setting, help to promote and extend thinking far more than low-level knowledge questions in which the pupil has a 50 per cent chance of being right: for example, 'Is salt a solid or a liquid?' compared with: 'If aliens landed on earth and wanted to know what a solid was how would you describe the properties of a solid so that they understood?'

Analytical questions require pupils to discuss how things are the same and different or what are the major causes of the event. For example:

Q: *'Does sugar dissolve?'*

A: *'No'*

can be replaced with

Q: *'What are the differences between melting and dissolving?'*

A: *'Melting is where the stuff changes shape, it goes runny and watery and a bit melty, but dissolving the stuff will go into the water so you can not see it. Melting you can see but dissolving you can not.' (Joseph, Year 6)*

Synthesis questions start from the premise that pupils can think for themselves, and link ideas together. For example, a group of Year 6 pupils were looking at 'Instant snow' which expands when water is added. They thought originally that the powder would dissolve, so were rather surprised by their observations. They thought that if you added more water it would dissolve and, so, a small amount was added to a large amount of water. It was still possible to see the granules.

Q: *'Based on your idea that when materials dissolve they are too small to see, can you explain if this is an example of dissolving?' (Teacher)*

A: *'You can still see the small bits of the stuff it is floating in the water. But if you add more water it will probably dissolve.' (Brett, Year 6)*

Q: *'Do you agree with Brett?' (Teacher)*

A: *'You can see the small bits but adding water will not make a difference it would have done it by now if it was going to. I think you could put it on an radiator in the sun and get it back so it's like dissolving because it will evaporate.' (Joseph, Year 6)*

The synthesis questions are ones that prompt pupils to see links and enables the teacher to plan the next steps in their learning as a result of talking to learn. Synthesis questions are very helpful and are typified as *so based on this fact what would your conclusions be?* type questions.

It is also important to allow opportunities for pupils to experience *evaluative questions*, which enable them to rank statements. For example, using the idea cards in Figure 4.1 the pupils had to decide which definition they agreed most with or make up one of their own.

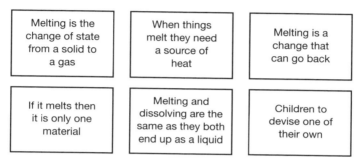

Figure 4.1 *Evaluative questions*

It is also important to include some *interpretive questions*, which require an opinion. This is required in many other high-level responses to questions. But is a useful strategy for responses, which are scientifically inaccurate. So when the pupil suggested, 'Dissolving is when it disappears or disintegrates' (Libby, Year 6), this response was answered with a question to the groups, 'Why would you agree with this statement?' thus allowing thinking time and responses from the groups with the teacher taking the role to move learning forward rather than being controlling.

Whatever range of strategies are used there is safety in numbers for the pupils. Using talking pairs is helpful but ensuring that the pairs are changed every two weeks is vital. Linking Talk pairs into Thoughtful fours (two pairs of pupils asked to consider ideas in a thoughtful way) can ensure a range of ideas are raised. Although calling out and putting hands up occurs in some classrooms, this practice means that only a few pupils have to 'do the work'. The hands-up strategy also leaves the problem of the pupils who do not have to take part. Traditional questioning with hands up and 'egg-laying sounds' is found to be detrimental to the development of thinking and is a type of neural pruning. If the brain is not used effectively its ability to make links is reduced. But when wait time is increased, response partners are used and the quality of questioning is improved, pupils make thoughtful responses and become more involved in their learning. Neural branching is an outcome of effective questioning.

Using Pupils' Questions as a Starting Point

Teachers should aim to use pupils' questions as often as possible for a number of varied reasons. Questioning as a process skill is an important part of the scientific process. As Smith and Peacock (1995, p.14) state, 'learning to ask good questions is an essential ingredient for science' and, in the long term a scientifically literate person needs to be an effective questioner, someone who can use their knowledge and understanding alongside the ability and confidence to ask the right question at the right time. Primary-aged pupils are living in an uncertain world where being able to question the world around them is increasingly important. Therefore it is important to encourage pupils' questions within formal education today.

Pupils' Questions

Pre-school children naturally raise many 'why' questions. This is typified in the book *Why* (Camp and Ross, 2000), a story of Lily and her father, who becomes increasingly exasperated trying to answer Lily's incessant 'why' questions. Experience tells us that 'why' questions are asked when children do not understand something, or when they need either to gain further information or to extend their knowledge of a familiar subject, or sometimes merely to gain attention from adults.

Although 'why' questions are important for developing pupils' knowledge and understanding of science, they are not the most important for providing opportunities to develop science process skills. Starting from pupils' own questions can provide some ownership of their own learning and, consequently, can be a terrific motivator. It is crucial that pupils do not merely undertake practical activities to reinforce existing ideas or to illustrate a concept. Whilst illustrative activities are important, it is also most important for pupils to explore and investigate practically things they do not know about. Merely following questions that pupils already know the answer to could lead to disaffection characterised by unwelcome questions such as 'why are we doing this?' However, if investigations are based on pupils' own real questions then the outcome will not be known before the exploration, research or investigation begins.

Furthermore, pupils' questions can also be a focus for formative assessment, not only to assess what pupils know or, more importantly, do not know, but also to provide an opportunity for teachers to assess the quality of their question-raising ability.

Answering Children's Questions

Pupils do need to ask questions to obtain information and to clarify unclear thinking. Many of the 'why' questions pupils ask can be easily answered by reference to textbooks set at the appropriate level. Children are fascinated by questions that ask, for example, about the tallest tree, the shortest man, etc. However, merely providing pupils with the 'correct' answer will rarely provide the long-term solution. Clearly, though, it would not be realistic, or appropriate, to expect teachers never to answer children's questions and teachers need to use their professional judgement when pupils ask questions. Before directly answering a pupil's question, teachers need to consider if doing so is in the best interest of the learner? Sometimes, as discussed above, it is appropriate to throw the question over to their peers, as other pupils can often offer an answer that is set at the appropriate level using more child-centred language or that provides a new slant that will enable more discussion to occur.

Instead of always being provided with the answer, pupils need to be taught to ask their own questions as a way of obtaining information and understanding in science. Pupils also need to recognise that for some questions, there is no known answer and that there are various ways of finding out the answers to different kinds of questions. Older pupils also need to learn how to make their initial questions into ones that can be investigated so they can find an answer by practical scientific enquiry. In order to learn this skill, pupils need time and the opportunity, built into their learning time, to consider what sorts of questions are suitable for answering by practical enquiry. Some ideas for developing this further are provided in Chapter 5.

By helping children to clarify, qualify and refine the question, the teacher's role is actually enhanced. Throwing the problem back to the pupil, asking 'What makes you ask that?' or 'What do you mean by that?', may well lead to more meaningful, longer-term learning than directly answering the question when the provided answer may or may not match the understanding of the learner. It is a common occurrence, even in adulthood, to be put off asking further questions because the answer to an initial question, even if accurate, was not understood. Answering pupils' questions at the correct level, with differentiation is a very difficult instructional skill and, more often than not, it is probably in the best interests of the learner if they are required to find out for themselves.

Helping Pupils to Raise Questions

In order to help pupils to develop their question-raising ability, teachers need to listen to the pupils' questions, analysing them to try to discover the reason for the question and whether or not they can be answered by practical enquiry. One of the most useful ways of promoting the questions that can lead to further practical enquiry is to provide pupils with the opportunity to explore and observe some objects, using all the senses (where appropriate). Older pupils can be given a simple resource and asked to ask questions about it. One Year 6 class provided with a potato as a stimulus raised 98 different questions. The teacher said that the questions ranged from 'Where did the original potato come from?' to 'How can we grow a potato?' So successful is this strategy that it is almost possible to base a whole term's cross-curricular work on the questions raised – very much in keeping with the current trend towards more cross-curricular work! Whilst the same range of questions may not be possible for all starting points, experience suggests that the latent potential of pupils raising their own questions may well be enormous. One strategy that helps pupils to raise questions is the use of a question hand (Figure 4.2).

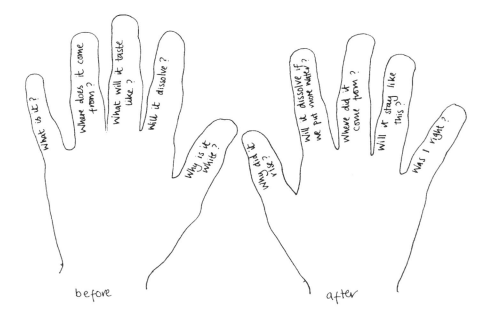

Figure 4.2 *The question hand*

Pupils were provided with some white powder (instant snow) in a transparent plastic cup and asked to think of questions they could ask about this and write them on their first hand. Then they were asked to add water to the powder and to observe what happened and to ask some more questions on their second hand. All pupils asked 10 questions, many of which could have been answered using a practical activity. It was interesting that the quality of the questions improved greatly after the water was added.

Children looking at small animals

There is often a tendency for teachers to ask pupils to research, prior to their exploration, the sorts of animals they may encounter in their local environment. The argument used to justify this strategy is that pupils will then be more informed about the animals they are likely to encounter before finding them. However, whilst important, knowing the name of an animal is not the most important reason for observing them. Preparing pupils in this way is tantamount to putting the cart before the horse in terms of learning because, inevitably, pupils are likely to notice those features that they have been prepared to notice, rather than observing features in an open-minded way (see Chapter 3). Pupils' questioning ability and their knowledge and understanding of small animals can be extended if they are challenged to notice similarities and differences between animals whilst observing them, then they will not only begin to appreciate the wide diversity of living things, but will also develop the scientific skill of classification of invertebrates. This will be particularly so if they are encouraged to use classification keys to identify the animals they come across.

When pupils are given the opportunity to observe a number of small animals it is almost impossible to stop them from asking questions about them. If they are asked to observe collected material for a few minutes, then to view the individuals, one at a time, in a viewer, they become fascinated. It is easy, for pupils working in pairs, to record their questions, either in writing or on tape, and then to seek answers to their questions. This strategy is particularly motivating because pupils themselves have ownership of the questions they ask and require little formal input from the teacher.

One reason why this activity can be such a good vehicle for raising questions is that pupils will immediately compare the animal to themselves and, amongst the many 'why' questions, there will be more productive questions such as:

- What is it?

- What does it eat?

- How does it feed?

- How many legs has it got?

- What are the feelers for?

- Does it have eyes?

- Is it a boy or a girl?

- Is this a baby one of these?

Teachers can prompt pupils, through questioning, into noticing missed features that are important to learning. Then pupils can choose some of the questions that they would really like to be answered either through looking again more closely, using secondary sources or by setting up a practical situation to try to find the answer to the question. Whilst consulting secondary sources looking for the answers to specific questions, pupils invariably not only find answers to questions that they had not even asked, but also begin to realise that some questions cannot easily be answered.

Of course, teachers need to provide a variety of resources and also to be aware themselves of which questions should be answered in a practical way, for example: 'What does the animal eat?', 'Under what conditions does it prefer to live?' or 'How far does the animal travel in five minutes?', etc. Teachers also need to know how these *could* be carried out practically, then, without giving too much information, they should scaffold the pupils so they can go about finding the answers to their questions. For a successful outcome, secondary resources set at an appropriate level need to be readily available for use by the pupils. It is important here to be aware that some well-known and recently published materials may unintentionally transmit misconceptions. For example, one book of insects contains spiders and another aimed at the primary age range has a large heading of 'Insects' on the cover with a much smaller heading of 'and other small creatures that live in the soil' with large pictures of a variety of groups of small animals on both the back and front cover of the book.

One of the best things about approaching this topic in an open-ended 'child-directed' way starting with questions is that it is highly likely that the questions asked by pupils will follow curriculum guidance. Not only are pupils introduced to the wide variety of living things by using such an approach, but also they are highly likely to explore the seven life processes of living things, namely, movement, reproduction, sensitivity, nutrition, respiration, growth and, though not in the statutory National Curriculum at Key Stages 1 or 2, excretion – a topic very much of interest to children! In working in this way pupils are very motivated and this suggests that the teaching style adopted has an effect on pupil learning, which is not seen with a list drawn up by the teacher. This approach still requires intervention by the teacher, not to direct learning in a formal way, but to ask the questions that pupils have not asked themselves.

Bubbles

Playing with bubbles is a common play activity both inside the early years classroom and outside. Bubbles fascinate learners of all ages. They provide a wonderful starting point for simple investigations arising out of observation. The beauty of using bubbles as a starting point for simple observational activities is that a whole series of activities based on simple observation can be completed in a few minutes. When starting with all resources for exploration, it is important that teachers have explored the possibilities for themselves, before the activity is carried out with pupils. It is also important to note that the learning outcomes here relate to process skill objectives and not, except incidentally, to those relating to knowledge and understanding.

Observing and Raising Questions about Bubbles

The example in Table 4.1 shows the types of questions that teachers can use not only to encourage further observation, but also to model the kinds of questions that can be investigated practically. Initially pupils should be provided with a pot of bubble mixture and bubble wands of various shapes and sizes. Once they have begun to explore blowing bubbles the possibilities for simple investigations arising out of frequently unstated questions are almost endless. The most important thing here is for the teacher not to ask questions too soon, or too quickly. Initially, it is better to watch what the pupils are doing and to listen to what they are saying and to take the questioning from the pupils, rather that to have a predetermined list of questions that *have* to be delivered. Observations and explorations need to be built upon rather than superimposing a set diet of activity on the pupils.

After just a few minutes pupils can share their observations with the rest of the class. Some pupils will have focused on some aspects and not noticed others. Sharing observations here allows a much wider number of observations and simple investigations to be undertaken in a relatively short time.

Pupils' observations or statements	Teacher questions
	What have you noticed about the bubble?
The bubble is coloured	What colour is a bubble? How many colours can you see? What do the colours remind you of?
The bubble is round	Are all bubbles the same shape? What shape is a bubble? What shape is the bubble as you blow through the frame? Can you blow a square bubble?
The bubbles float	What happens if you use different size bubble frames? Can you make it touch the ceiling? Will it stay in the air forever? How long can you get it to stay off the ground? What do you think is inside the bubble? How is it different from the bubble mixture? Does it float up or down? Why do you think it moved that way? How did you make it move that way?
I can blow a big bubble	What happens to the size of the bubble when you blow slowly? What happens to the size of the bubble when you blow quickly? In which ways are big and small bubbles the same and in which ways are they different?
The bubble popped	What is the shape of the popped bubble? How long did the bubble last? Can you count how many seconds the bubble lasted before it popped? If the bubble was made out of a different material would it still pop?
Look, two bubbles bumped into each other	What happens to the shape of bubbles when two bubbles join together? How many bubbles can you make stick together? Magnets attract some metals do you think this is the same? What shape can you see inside the bubble?
I can see reflections	What can you see in the reflections? Are the reflections the right way up? Can your bubble make a shadow? How do a shadow and a reflection differ?
It is dripping	What words can you use to describe the bubble now? Could you get a dry bubble?

Table 4.1 *Teacher questions to aid observation and promote simple investigations*

Progression in Children Raising Questions

Case Study 4.1: Children's Questions about bread

Bread is a very good starting point for scientific investigations and has the additional attraction of providing a multicultural dimension. What follows is a case study account of the response of four pupils, two girls and two boys each from Year R, Year 2, Year 4 and Year 6. All pupils were provided with the same starting point, a variety of 'breads' from around the world to explore, to observe using all the senses and to raise questions about the different breads. The breads provided were:

- Baguette: typical French bread
- Pitta bread: unleavened bread that can be split open to hold a filling
- Chapatti: flat 'bread' with obvious herbs within it
- Naan bread: leavened Indian bread in a flattened tear-drop shape
- Mediterranean roll: a very colourful, rich bread with identifiable pieces of olive and tomato within it
- Stay fresh white bread: 'long life'
- Ciabatta: flattish Italian bread made with olive oil
- Wholemeal brown bread: traditional sliced brown bread.

Initially all the pupils from each year group were asked what they noticed about the different breads at the exploration stage. If necessary they were then prompted with the following questions:

- What do you think it tastes like?
- What does it smell like?
- What does it look like?
- What might you eat with it?
- Where do you think it comes from?
- When would you eat it?
- Do you know what sort of bread it is?

Pupils were asked to:

- look at the bread
- think of any words to describe the bread
- choose one type of bread to draw
- to ask any questions about the bread. (The question hand was used again.)

▶

All pupils were most interested in the Mediterranean bread, the chapatti and the naan bread. Of all the breads, the Mediterranean bread was the least familiar bread and white bread and wholemeal bread the most familiar.

Pupils' observations of Mediterranean bread, and activities that could follow

Year group	Children's observations	Activities that could follow from the observations
Foundation Stage	Tended not to comment about the bread, but their observational drawings suggested that they had noticed 'bits' of black pieces of olive and red pieces of tomato within the bread.	The 'bits' could have been taken from the bread, put in piles and weights of each could be compared using simple scales, to find the proportion of each.
Year 2	Looks like a current bun with cracks on it. It looks like it has raisins in it. It tastes fruity – very yummy. Pupils thought it came from a bakery in Dover.	Comparison of the olives and tomatoes with raisins by sight, touch and taste to see if the pupils' idea was correct. Finding out what was in the bread by comparison of simple possible ingredients.
Year 4	Jane notice that the bread 'smells like garlic' and noticed herbs and 'fruit' in it. She thought that its texture was 'quite squidgy' and tasted tomatoey like a pasta sauce and came originally from Italy.	It was interesting that Jane compared the taste of the bread to her experience of other food. She was trying to make sense of her observations. The smell of the bread could have been compared to a clove of garlic and a range of herbs used for baking.
Year 6	Mandy thought it had fruit inside and that the texture was hard, on the outside, but 'squidgey and lumpy on the inside'. She did not like the taste, describing it as disgusting because she detected the smell of garlic and herbs with the bread. Mandy commented that it was difficult to describe the smell. Egan thought that the bread probably came from Italy. Sam thought it looked brown and bumpy and that it felt hard and lumpy. He thought it tasted like a pasta sauce and thought that the bread came from Italy because pasta comes from Italy. Tim thought that the bread looked like a fruit cake, smelled like tomato puree, was hard and tasted a bit like a pizza and came from Italy.	The Year 6 pupils were much more sophisticated in their previous experience of foods and were able to correctly identify a number of tastes presented to them in the bread. They also had more understanding of the origin of various foodstuffs. However, they tended not to ask questions that could be investigated. Again though, these pupils could have explored further the proportion of ingredients and compared tastes to herbs that might have been in the bread. Acting like detectives, before looking on the bread packet.

Questions children asked about the bread

Inevitably, a number of questions were asked by pupils of all years that were not particularly productive in terms of leading to further observation or investigation in science. Examples of these included 'Where did the bread come from?' 'What is the name of the bread?' 'What country did the bread come from?' 'Have you ever been to the country where this bread comes from?' However, other questions were potentially more useful.

Questions leading to further practical work

Year	Question	Questions that could lead to further practical work
Year R	Notices the 'bits' in the bread	How many different 'bits' are there in the bread? What are the 'bits' in the bread?
Year 2	How is the bread made?	Making bread using ingredients listed on the packet.
Year 4	Why does the 'stay fresh' bread always stay fresh?	How long does 'stay fresh' bread stay fresh? Looking on the packet for the 'use by' date. Comparing bread packets to find out what ingredient helped to keep the bread fresher for longer. Setting up a practical situation (taking care to do this safely) to find out which bread, e.g. 'stay fresh', ordinary white bread and wholemeal bread, stays freshest for longest. Making bread using ingredients listed on packets (where possible). Omitting single ingredients systematically to find out what difference this makes to the bread.
	Why did the Mediterranean bread taste like 'Domino's' pizza?	What ingredients give the bread its characteristic smell? Comparing herbs in pots to smell of bread to try to determine the ingredients.
	Why has the naan bread got bits in it?	What would the naan bread taste like without the 'bits' in it? Finding out what the bits are and making naan bread without the 'bits.'
	Why is the baguette my favourite?	Survey of children's preferences of the breads under study.
Year 6	Why do you like it?	Survey of the reasons why pupils like different breads.
	Where does it come from?	Answers found by consulting secondary sources.
	What is special about it?	Comparing breads by further observation and looking at lists of ingredients from packets or recipe books.

▶

Why is it called chapatti?	Research of secondary sources.
What does it smell of?	Comparison of the smell of different breads.
What colour is it?	Describing the colour of different breads.
How would you describe it?	Asking pupils to describe bread.
How do you think it was made?	Looking up recipes and trying to make the bread.

Whilst most of the pupils involved in this case study knew what a question was, they were not very good at raising investigative questions. However, some questions could be derived from their spontaneous questions and some of these could lead to further observation or investigative work.

Summary

Pupils ask a wide variety of questions, but some of these are not as useful in promoting scientific enquiry as others. Observation works to encourage questioning because pupils are starting with things they notice and in which they are interested. The teacher's role in this process is to encourage observation, to ask pupils what they have noticed and to clarify questions.

Finally, it is important to know when and how to intervene when pupils ask questions. It is pertinent to note at this point that at the Foundation Stage teachers are warned that 'giving the game away' too early during an activity may limit the depth of children's learning; telling children before they have a chance to experience the 'eureka moment' provides information, but prevents the development of investigative skills (QCA, 2000, p.83). This message is true also of all teaching in science and the implication of this may well be far-reaching for many teachers in the primary classroom.

CHAPTER 5

Scientific Enquiry

Hellen Ward

Introduction

This chapter will highlight the difference between illustrative and investigative activities. The procedures involved in investigating an idea will be developed in sequence and illustrated with pupils' work where appropriate. Some suggested complete investigations will be provided and the chapter will conclude with a reminder that the fair test is only one type of investigation.

The Importance of Scientific Enquiry

The focus of science teaching has most recently centred upon the knowledge and understanding of science at the expense of investigative and illustrative processes because of the emphasis upon Year 6 pupils attaining Level 4 in national tests. As a result many pupils receive a very bland and boring diet of science involving comprehension tasks. In recent years the lack of investigative approaches has been commented upon in a number of forums from parliamentary reports (2003), OfSTED publications (OfSTED/HMI, 2002; 2003; 2004) and the professional press. Time pressure, a testing arrangement that appeared to favour what was 'easy to test' rather than 'what is science', together with the introduction of 'the National Primary Strategies', have all contributed to the current position. It is possible, indeed, there is an opportunity, that the changes to the tests initiated in 2003 might help to refocus science teaching.

Investigative work is more than any activity that involves equipment and practical tasks. Figure 5.1 denotes the stages of scientific enquiry. It can be seen that there are many steps, and when undertaking an investigation the pupils will follow and be involved in all the steps. In illustrative work steps 1–5 will be undertaken by the teacher. This is perhaps why pupils make so many predictions as this is the first part of the process where they can be involved. Basic skill lessons focus on only one step at a time, as discussed in detail in Chapter 2.

1. Selection of the global question*
2. Identification of the independent variables
3. Thinking of how to measure/observe the outcome (dependent variable)
4. Question generation
5. Selecting the equipment and deciding how to use it
6. Deciding what might happen (making a prediction) if needed*
7. Data collection methods – type and amount of data to be collected*
8. Making observations and measurements
9. Recording and evaluating the data (reliability)
10. Interpreting the data
11. Drawing conclusions
12. Evaluating the process*

*Using secondary sources of information can occur at a number of points. It will differ according to the investigation as well as age of pupils, but is an important part of the process.

Figure 5.1 *The stages of scientific enquiry*

The term 'investigation' is used explicitly for activities, which require pupils to think and make choices about 'what to vary' and 'what to measure'. It is this *choice* that is important as it enables the pupils to plan their own work. In investigative work pupils plan by selecting the variable (factor) they will change and then deciding how to measure and record the effect of the changes. The pupils then carry out the whole process of investigating their own idea, using basic skills they have acquired.

Illustrative work is important as it enables pupils to learn about science in a practical way by focusing upon a limited number of skills at any one time. Such work enables pupils to change or vary factors and to measure or observe effects, but the 'what to do' and the 'how to do it' is prescribed by the teacher. Illustrative science allows pupils to arrive at the expected outcome as it is teacher directed at most stages. Due to the formal nature of the illustration it is easy to focus pupils' attention directly upon what is required. The methods of communication and recording are also prescribed in illustrative work, and the activities undertaken provide experiences upon which future investigations can be based. Illustrative work provides opportunities for pupils to experience aspects of scientific enquiry.

It is a myth that pupils will become investigative scientists by a process similar to osmosis, picking up skills, attitudes and concepts by 'being there'! Pupils generate ideas and questions but enabling them to answer these questions in a

Key Stage 1

Aspects	Reception	Year 1	Year 2
Methods of working	Work is totally supported by adult	Beginning to work in groups supported by adults	Groups working on own investigations supported by planning format and class teachers
Question formation	Adult generates questions	Adult sets question. Pupils begin to raise own questions	Questions and suggestions made by pupils and they respond to teacher questions
Prediction	Pupils formulate idea/ guess in head. Pupils are not asked "what will happen?"	Pupils are asked as a result of their work whether what happened was what was expected	Pupils are asked if what happened was expected and to give some reasons
Variables	Teacher selects variables i.e. type of material, amount of water	Teacher and pupils select variables i.e. types of material, amount of water, type of liquid	Teacher and pupils brainstorm variables then pupils choose e.g. types of material, amount of water, type of liquid, amount of material
Range and Interval	Range selected by teacher	Simple range discussed by pupils and teachers. Interval set by the teacher	Range developed by the pupils i.e. three materials chosen. Interval discussed where relevant i.e. 0ml water, 50ml water, 100ml water
Choosing and Using Equipment	Everyday objects used, provided by teacher. Used with some support	Some everyday objects and simple equipment, sand timers, straws (non-standard measure) selected with limited support	Independent usage of simple equipment provided by teacher i.e. metre sticks, scales, tape measure
Observations and Measurements	Simple observations made i.e. wet/dry	Beginning to use non –standard measurements and to talk about their observations	Some use of standard units to measure length, mass. More than one reading beginning to be made. Observations used to make comparisons
Oral Communication	Pupils respond to questions about their work. They are able to talk in sentences relating two events together	Pupils begin to talk about whether what happened was what they expected	Pupils make comparisons "this cloth was more absorbent than that one". Some simple reasons are given
Written Communication	No written feedback expected. Emergent writing or Q and A by adult represents work	Simple writing to convey meaning used to communicate findings e.g. a letter to Alex's mum	Writing used to describe what happened. Scientific knowledge and understanding is developed through conclusion
Graphical Representation	Charts modelled by teacher begun to be drawn by pupils	Tables (2 columns) and charts produced by pupils with limited support. Bar charts are modelled by adult	Tables with space for a repeat reading introduced. Pupils draw bar charts. Adult helps with scale if appropriate. Patterns and trends are discussed as a class
Scientific Vocabulary	Simple words. Adult models correct vocabulary i.e. hard, soft, smooth	Vocabulary extended. Adults are still modelling. Displays provide important reinforcement	Pupils use simple vocabulary to explain results. Adult modelling and displays still very important. Concept maps/ kwhl grids develop vocabulary
Health & Safety	Follows simple instructions when carrying out activities	Follows instructions when using equipment. Can respond to adult questions about safe working	Know about safe and careful working. Following instructions. Emphasis still on teacher to control hazards and risks

Table 5.1a *Progression of procedural understanding*

Key Stage 2

Aspects	Year 3	Year 4	Year 5	Year 6
Methods of working	Individual work within a group with some support by adult	Teacher supports occasionally when needed. Pupils work in groups	Group working mainly unsupported.	No support for groups in normal situations. Scaffolds removed
Question formation	After class brainstorms of global question. Pupils start to raise own questions	Questions selected by pupils global question starts process.	Opportunities are given for pupil questions to be followed as a result of an initial investigation	A range of questions is tested as a result of own ideas that arise from work. Not just of fair test variety
Prediction	Predictions are made with encouragement. Predictions include a reason	Level 3 predictions beginning to include knowledge and understanding	Predictions draw on past experience. Simple knowledge and understanding is used	Predictions are developed and explanations of these use sound understanding of area covered
Variables	Pupils with support, identify a range of variables that could be tested i.e. height, weight, material, size, way it is dropped, length of wing. Standard units are introduced	Pupils identify variables with limited support i.e. amount of soil, type of soil, amount of water, temperature of water	Scaffold used independently and a wide range of variables are identified i.e. type of substance, amount of liquid, size of container, amount of sugar, temperature of water, type of liquid, stir or not	Variables are identified by pupils and are chosen and manipulated ensuring a fair test if appropriate
Range and Interval	Pupils begin to understand the need range. Range chosen suits investigations i.e. 3 helicopters. Interval developed with help of teacher but is still non-standard i.e. small, medium and large	Range understood. Numbers used varies according to context but a minimum of 4 i.e. 4 types of soil, materials. Interval identified by pupils but still non-standard i.e. coarse, fine, thin materials	Range used independently and 5 or more are used routinely. The interval contains standard measurements and is systematically selected with some limited support from peers and teacher	Pupils use appropriate range to enable patterns and trends to be identified (6 as minimum). Pupils use K & U to identify appropriate intervals in a systematic way. Standard units are selected
Choosing and Using Equipment	Using simple equipment with some support eg thermometer, Newton meter, stop watch	Using equipment confidently with limited support to nearest whole number	Know what equipment to use selecting it themselves. Careful and correct usage to1N, 1gm, 1mm, 1cm^3	Self-selecting from using past experience. Range of equipment selected for a range of tasks. Repeated measurements taken which are precise
Observations and Measurements	Simple observations used and measurements (3) accompany these. S.I. units of measurement for T°C, time, force	Three or more measurements taken routinely. S.I. units used with care. Scanning for unusual readings introduced	Dependent on context multiple readings become part of procedure. Unusual readings are discussed and repeated if time allows	Multiple measurements taken (6+). These are accurate. Unusual results are repeated automatically
Oral Communication	Teachers use feedback session to develop oral skills. Events described in order	Pupils report back with limited support. Teacher questioning used to develop explanations.	Teacher's role is to prompt when descriptions not explanations are given. Teachers and pupils ask questions to develop K and U. Systematic concise style encouraged.	Pupils report back including all relevant details. Explain what they found out and how they could improve their investigations. Teacher's role is as audience
Written Communication	Teacher models appropriate responses. Simple writing frame supports simple conclusions. Patterns and trends are written about. "What did it mean?" is more important than "what I did"	Explanations encouraged through written work. Patterns and trends developed. Questions "Did the evidence support the prediction?" "What do I know now that was not known before?"	Method, apparatus conclusions are NOT recommended. Explanations are given, patterns and trends are discussed. Generalisations are included. Scaffolding is reduced	Scaffolding is reduced/ removed. Conclusions draw on scientific K and U, the predictions and the evidence

Graphical Representation	Tables - 3 measurements and * (star) column are drawn unaided. Total or median is used. Bar charts produced unaided. Teacher helps pupils to identify the patterns and trends	Tables constructed unaided. Pupils check for unusual results with adults. Median used. Bar graphs constructed unaided. Patterns and trends discussed with limited support	Tables are sophisticated. Averages used. Unusual results discussed. Line graphs are drawn which have a few points and whole number scales. Decision about line/ bar graph or scattergraph made in consultation with teacher	Tables are clearly presented. Average used where appropriate. Consolidation of line graphs, bar charts and scatter grams. These have more points and complex scales. IT is used effectively. These graphical representations are used to draw results. Scientific vocabulary
Scientific Vocabulary	Vocabulary used to develop concepts. Correct vocabulary used to explain observations. Comparisons used effectively. KWHL grids/ concept maps start process off	Correct vocabulary i.e. dissolving, melting, evaporating is used by teacher in course of work. Differences between the definitions of scientific words developed. Scientific vocabulary used as matter of course	Simple generalization explained using correct vocabulary. Definitions of words used given by pupils i.e. gravity. Questioned by adults/ peers. KWHL grids/ concept maps still used as starting point	Scientific vocabulary used effectively to develop generalisations. KWHL grids /concept maps compared by pupils and definitions for words explained. Terms used effectively i.e. melting, dissolving, evaporating, condensing and in a range of contexts
Health & Safety	Knows term hazard and risk. Begins to use terms while assessing 'dangers' in practical work	Develops idea of recognising hazards and risks in investigative work. Can respond to questions	Begin to assess hazards and risks in their own work without prompts. Beginning to take action to control risks	Controls hazards and risks. Demonstrates in their work that they understand concept of hazard and risk

Table 5.1b *Progression of procedural understanding*

scientific way requires procedural understanding to be developed throughout the primary age range. The process should be started in the early years and the degree of challenge and the complexity of tasks increased as pupils progress through the school. In order to be successful there needs to be a common approach across the school, with all adults working in similar ways. This is known as continuity, and without a continuous approach it is unlikely that pupils' learning will progress. In order to make this easier to manage there needs to be agreement about progression in procedural understanding which will result in all teachers knowing what pupils have already been taught and where they are expected to progress next. This is easier to achieve if the expectation for ways of working in all aspects of science are clearly stated for each year group. From a simple starting point in early years, pupils will develop more independence. The level descriptions (Attainment Target 1) make it clear where progress should be focused at each level through the key stages. Using this information together with extensive opportunities to work with pupils in whole-class investigative activities and in real settings allowed a suggested framework for progression to be constructed. Table 5.1 (a) and (b) provide an opportunity for teachers to gain an understanding of where the age range they teach fits within the whole schemata and is a starting point for future discussion in schools.

The theory supporting this framework has as the central tenet that pupils will make gains in understanding and skills, if development is in small steps and there is support from teachers and others. For pupils to be successful, teachers have continually to aim to extend unaided achievement, by planning small steps and increasing the challenge. This is only effective when all teachers work to the same goals and realistic but challenging expectations are set from the start. It also requires a belief in the importance of procedural understanding.

Methods of Working

Young children have their own ideas and are keen to find out about the world. When pupils start school the whole process of investigation should begin with the teacher supporting the work at all stages. A suitable idea can be generated from work already occurring in the classroom. Sometimes this can result from a suggestion made by a pupil or it might be teacher directed: the teacher models the investigative approach with the same variable being investigated by all the pupils. By Year 2, pupils will have experience of a number of investigations. They will be used to working in groups and of being supported by the teacher and their peers. They will be used to identifying variables from a global question and will be able to think of a question their group can answer. The pupils will at this age begin to take a more independent role and build upon the skills and experiences gained earlier in the key stage. The teachers/adults have an important role here in facilitating the work but not leading it. In Key Stage 2 the process should be further developed, with teachers supporting not directing. It is found to be most effective if direct adult support is reduced over time and with the reduction corresponding to the development of the pupils' skills and abilities. Thus the role of the teacher is to model and support the learning processes throughout.

Whatever type of investigation is planned the teacher must identify in advance, the variables possible and proposals for how and what data collection methods might be used. In investigative work pupils should be provided with some *choice* within this demarked activity. As already stated in Chapter 2, trying to 'shoe horn' a fair test into a survey will result in strange results and confuse teachers and pupils.

Question Formulation

In order to begin to investigate, an idea or a question is needed to stimulate thinking. With younger pupils this process is new and, therefore, modelling and scaffolding at all stages is essential. Selecting a simple global question that results in few variables, where there are clear outcomes (results) and the context is related to real life is central to success at this age. In Early Years classrooms because adults provide the global questions and identify the variables to test, the focus is on providing opportunities to introduce the pupils to the processes involved in testing out ideas. By Year 2, pupils will be able to respond to the global question and begin to identify variables themselves. The teacher will at this stage still be supporting the process. However, by Year 6, pupils should be able to think of their own questions as a result of ideas developed from illustrative tasks.

Identification of Variables

In the initial stages it is necessary to use a planning format (Figure 5.2) to support both teachers and pupils. This modelling is necessary because it makes explicit that which is implicit in the process of investigating an idea. A range of types of scaffolds should be used, which increase in complexity throughout the primary years and many are based upon an original idea by Goldsworthy (1997). Pictorial clues, pictures of objects to change or measure rather than only written words, are used with young pupils wherever possible as a way of communicating effectively.

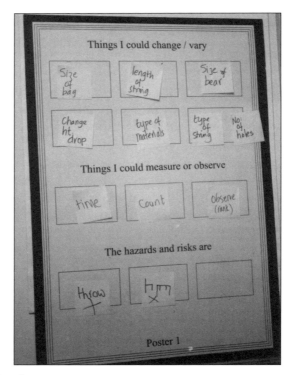

Figure 5.2 *Planning format*

With older pupils the range of variables is identified by the pupils. Figure 5.3 demonstrates variables identified by a class of Year 4 pupils investigating the global question 'Which factors effect the time a parachute is in the air?' The pupils were shown two parachutes of different sizes. The pupils had not taken part in a complete investigation prior to this lesson, but were able to brainstorm all the factors in less than five minutes.

Group work

Pupils should work in small group situations from Reception onwards. However, in the Early Years the activity is likely to be tackled by the pupils individually taking turns, rather than as a co-operative working group. What is important is the opportunity for pupils to be introduced to practices, which will be refined throughout the key stages. There is no requirement that all groups should work at the same time, and the investigation could be a teacher-directed small group task, if this suits the learning needs of the pupils or overall plans.

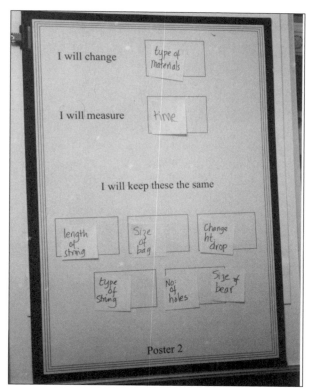

Figure 5.3 *Photograph of parachute variables*

Later in the key stage, for time management and learning reasons, it is more effective for all pupils to work at the same time. By Key Stage 2 the expectation is that all pupils work in groups at the same time and the class shares conclusions at the end of the session.

Equipment Selection

Whilst it is clear that pupils at Key Stage 1 should work with materials and equipment provided for them, this is inappropriate for pupils at the top end of the school. However, it is difficult for pupils to select equipment if they are unsure of what to use and have little or no previous experience of working unaided. This is where continuous practice is needed and clear expectations essential. If many illustrative tasks are used throughout the unit of work, which then culminates in a complete investigation, pupils are more aware of the choice of, and ways to use equipment. However, if the investigation is not linked to other areas of work, showing pupils a selection of resources that can be used is important. Initially this could be by starting the investigation with a 'Blue Peter here is one I made earlier' example, so that the pupils have a visual starting point provided along with the global question. Having resources set out around the room that are discussed with the pupils is also important, as is including some inappropriate equipment for older pupils. As age and confidence increase then greater resource choices should be provided allowing pupils to build upon skills learnt through illustrative lessons.

It is recommended that pupils draw the equipment they need. This process is a vital part of planning because by drawing the equipment, pupils are thinking about and rehearsing the activity at the same time. Scientists plan and record what they are going to do, in order to think through the process and so that after the event others can follow their methods. This is the same for pupils although it will be the teacher, parents or Ofsted inspectors rather than the public at large that look at their work. Pupils' illustrated plans enable assessments of their understanding to be made prior to the investigation beginning. Examples of childrens' plans are shown on the website (www.paulchapmanpublishing.co.uk\resources\ward.pdf). There is no requirement for early years pupils to plan their work in this way as they will be using equipment and questions provided by their teachers. The focus for this age range is the development of charts.

Predictions

The requirement to predict what will happen is not needed at Key Stage 1. However, at the start of Key Stage 2 pupils can be asked to place a tick on their plan to demonstrate the aspect they believe will be most effective. Pupils are also encouraged to give a reason for their choice. Predicting is not needed in every investigation but it does provide some indication of ideas and understanding being used in tandem with skills. If younger pupils spontaneously state what they think will happen, this should be written on their work. All pupils should be asked at the end of their work to reflect upon whether what happened was what they had expected and, although this requirement is explicitly Level 2, it is good practice for it to be included for all pupils.

Observations and Measurements

It is expected that younger pupils will observe events rather than measure or compare them. Observations will still be important at Key Stage 2 particularly in those aspects of science where measurement is difficult (e.g. the brightness of bulbs in circuit work or the loudness of sound). New equipment, in the form of sensors, is now available and found in many schools. These should be used to obtain standard units of measurement wherever possible. Recording standard units of measurement should be the norm for most investigations in Key Stage 2 and as pupils move through the school there should be an increase in the expected demand. Pupils independently should be able to identify any measurements that are unusual, take precise readings and by the end of the primary phase take repeat readings. Making observations and taking accurate measurements results from teaching basic skills and from practice, while the understanding of what to, and how many, measures or observations to make are part of planning.

Tables, Charts and Graphs

Even the youngest pupils are capable of creating a simple chart with help. Drawing the chart is a skill and thus can be modelled to the whole class, and then additional support provided for those pupils who have difficulty with this form of representation; interestingly, such pupils often have difficulties later with drawing graphs. At these early stages it is important that the charts are very simple and directly related to the activity. For example, if the activity is to find a material suitable for an umbrella, a sample of each of the materials to be tested can be stuck into the chart, because drawings and other representations are too difficult for many pupils at this stage.

Whilst it is important for the adults to understand the progression of the skills of enquiry, this can also be communicated to the pupils by changing the scaffolds that are in use. An example is provided for constructing tables (Figure 5.4.). This shows progression from simple charts to two-column tables (2 C tables) and eventually to tables that can include a range of measurements and observations.

There is no expectation that young pupils will construct their own graphs. It is important to note that time spent with young children constructing pictograms can sometimes contribute to problems with graphs at a later stage, i.e. numbers drawn in the boxes, etc. By Year 2 pupils should be able to draw their own simple bar graph with limited support relating to the selection of scale. By Year 6 pupils should be confident enough to draw line and scatter graphs. It is important that these skills are initially developed outside the framework of investigations. Many investigations falter at this point because without graphs pupils are unable to complete the process as they cannot identify clear patterns and trends from which to draw conclusions.

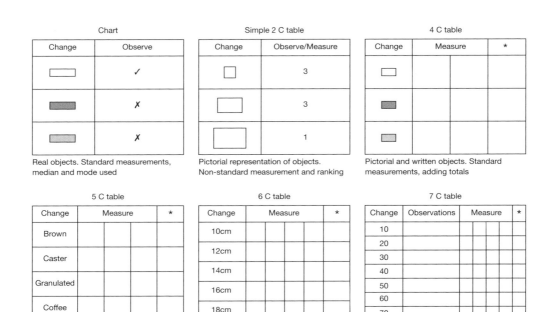

Figure 5.4 *Table development scaffolds*

Communicating Results and Concluding

When communicating findings, pupils need to be provided with many opportunities and styles. How the results are communicated should vary according to the age of the pupils as well as the enquiry type, as discussed in Chapter 2. Whilst young pupils are developing their ability to use written language, an approach focused completely upon this mode will be unsuccessful. When the observational part of an activity is completed, the work should be discussed orally and the outcomes shared visually; making a wall display or putting some outcomes into a class 'scrap book' celebrates this work.

A scrapbook, where different pupils take turns to record the investigative work throughout the year, records and monitors the development of science for the class. As a specialised task for individuals to complete, it also provides an opportunity for teachers to focus upon individuals at a set time. Many ways of teaching the skills of concluding and explaining findings were also suggested in Chapter 2. In complete investigations pupils should be enabled to demonstrate their skills. Pupils who find written responses difficult should be supported and provided with prompts to help their writing. Writing frames became *de rigueur* in many schools at the height of the literacy strategy, however, providing the same scaffold at the end of each investigation limits motivation and creativity.

Creativity occurs when time and choice are provided. This was demonstrated by a Year 1 child investigating the global question 'how to keep teddy dry'. She used all the materials she had tested to make a collage of the teddy, with the umbrella made of foil, the material that she had found to be waterproof. In addition, she had stuck a flap on her work, which when lifted had the word foil written underneath. Her response took no longer than any other child's but was even more outstanding as this was the first lesson in the term where she completed a lesson in an appropriate manner.

Writing a letter to explain results is effective, especially if the letters are posted and responses are received. Survey investigations such as the washing-up liquid producing the most bubbles, the strongest kitchen towel, the most effective toothpaste or strongest tea bags offer great opportunities for letter writing. Not all conclusions have to be written, pictures can convey meaning and adults can ask questions and scribe responses for future reference. News reports and role play enable pupils to demonstrate their understanding, which is the main point of concluding and explaining the results. Picture boards and story boards also make excellent communication strategies as does *telling* the story of the investigation.

Suitable Complete Investigations

Selecting a clear global question is fundamental to the success of the whole process of complete investigations. Equally important is identifying the variables from which pupils can select. Table 5.2 provides some ideas of investigations for the whole primary age range. This is not an exhaustive list, but all investigations that are suggested here have been tried and tested in a number of settings and are activities that pupils and teachers have enjoyed.

Investigation context and global questions	Independent variables	Dependent variable	Year group	Notes
Sc3 How can we keep Teddy dry?	Types of materials Number of layers Amount of water Type of liquid	Whether Teddy wet or dry (✓ or X) Can be developed into ranking using an arbitrary scale 4–1	Reception or Year 1 as there are few variables and it is direct observations	Great from a story start. Droppers are good to use
Sc3 Which material will make the longest snake?	Type of material, size of material, how it is stretched (pulled, rolled or flattened) Where it is rolled?	Length of snake – observation and ranking. Standard measure with cm	Year 1, as few measurements needed and results can be scaffolded by adults into a graph	Opportunity to develop simple comparison and measurement. Also reliability can be introduced as the results between girls and boys often vary greatly
Sc4 How can we give Teddy the longest ride?	Size of box, material on the bottom of box, size of bear, height of slope, number of bears, position of bears in box	Distance travelled in arbitrary units or cms. Use paper strips to measure distance to give immediate comparisons (bar charts) Observation and ranking.	Year 2 as this investigation will give opportunities to demonstrate Level 3	Less gender issues than cars down slopes and less discrete variables
Sc4 Which sounds travel the furthest?	Object dropped, material dropped onto surface, height of drop, force of drop	Number of steps away noise heard, distance sound heard in cm/m	Year 2 as opportunities for Level 3 and a challenging concept that enables some clear conclusions to be drawn	Care of feet and H&S for objects that are suitable to drop. Keep force of drop as a constant and always roll out of hand
Sc3 Which is the most absorbent kitchen towel?	Type of towel, size of towel, number of layers, amount of liquid, type of liquid	Observation of size of puddle left, amount of water in ml	Year 1 for observation, Year 2 for measurement of liquid	If observations of puddle then ensure the liquid has some food dye added to give easier visibility. If amount of water to be measured than place water into Petri dish
Sc2 Minibeasts survey Where will we find minibeasts?	Types of animal Place	Number/tally	Year 2	
Sc3 What materials should we use to make Alex's new clothes?	Type of material, number of layers, size of pieces tested Place tested. Size of stone, type of surface for rubbing	Number of rubs, observation after a set number of rubs (some children have tested for waterproofing as well)	Year 1 or 2 Easy to carry out as first investigation for Year 1 pupils. Opportunity for graph work and it is possible to produce Level 3 responses	Story start from 'New clothes for Alex'. Reporting back conclusions as a letter to Alex's mother works well

Table 5.2 *Some suggested investigations for primary schools*

Investigation context and global questions	Independent variables	Dependent variable	Year group	Notes
Sc3 Which are the strongest soaker uppers?	Type of kitchen towels. Amount of water, size of towels, number of layers	Number of masses (unit of 1 or 100gm)	Year 3 as measurement opportunities are suited to this age range	If no water is added then the towels will take 1.5kg. Recommended that 10ml of water used as minimum and that pupils are shown how to squirt water onto towel in slow and measured way
Sc3 Which ball bounces the most?	Type of ball, size of ball, type of surface, height of drop, way of letting go	Number of bounces, height of bounce, ranking against body	Year 2	Pupils bend knees to catch balls and a result this will affect measurement against body. It is vital to have a pair of "eyes" for this work
Sc2 Which washing powders are better for the environment?	Type of washing powder, amount of pond weed, amount of water, amount of powder, position of plants	Length of pond weed, colour and health of pond weed, judged on arbitrary scale	Year 6	Only pond weed collected from a fresh water fish supplier or recognised source must be used. It is not safe to use pond weed from the environment. Be careful with washing powders in the classroom and ensure no pupils can drink the solutions made
Sc 2 What will help cut flowers last longest?	Type of cut flower, type of flower additive, amount of water, temperature and position of plant, amount of plant additive	Length of time flowers last, change of water colour or smell, leaf/petal fall	Year 3	Old wives tales and ideas and evidence can be integrated into this investigation, as there are many homemade ideas of how to keep flowers for longer. Aspirin and other remedies should not be used without H&S assessments
Sc 2 Do all flowers change colour with food dye?	Type of flower, length of stem, amount of dye, number of cuts in stem, concentration of dye	Time taken to change colour. Observation and ranking of effect, Time taken to move 1 cm up stem	Year 5	Some plants will not work at all, and only food dye has an effect. Tulips are very fast whilst carnations work effectively in 4 hours. It is easy to dye flowers into quarters but patience is needed

Table 5.2 *Continued*

▶

Investigation context and global questions	Independent variables	Dependent variable	Year group	Notes
Sc3 What factors affect the behaviour of marble chips?	Type of liquid, amount of liquid, size of chip, position of activity, type of container	Time taken for marble to change size, (size over time), observation and ranking	Year 5	Ensure that a range of liquids are used including ones with opportunities to react with Carbonate. Do not make link between this and teeth as it is not a direct one and liquids that would encourage growth of plaque will not have any effect on marble!
Sc4 Which shoes would have more grip on an icy day?	Type of shoe, size of shoe, type of surface used, angle of surface, weight of shoe	Mass needed to move shoe, height/angle of slope, force in Newtons	Year 4	Easy and can be undertaken at a number of ages but use of force metre is linked with Year 4
Sc4 How to make a parachute that stays in the air for the longest time?	Size of parachute, type of material, shape of parachute, number of holes, weight (size of compare bear) length of string, thickness of string, ways of letting go, height dropped.	Time taken to hit the ground. Observation and ranking, counting of fall in seconds	Year 4	Use of shopping bags of different sizes works well. Attach bear with elastic band around its body and tie strings to this. Knot strings to corners of the bag. H&S plastic bags in classroom and lengths of string supervision needed
Sc3 Which are the most stretchy tights?	Type of tights, size of tights, type of mass, amount of mass	Length of tights, comparison, observation and ranking	Year 3	This needed a great deal of space or specifically brought tights. A fun activity that needs tall children. Small plastic bags of sand are useful
Sc4 What factors affect the property of a shadow?	Type of light source, type of object, distance of object from light source, distance of object from screen (wall) angle of light	Size of shadow Density of shadow	Year 4 or Year 6 dependent on outcome. This could become a complex Level 5 investigation	Data logging with light sensors is useful for this investigation as are hand held light metres
Sc3 Best bubble mixture	Type of washing liquid, amount of glycerine, time left, amount of water (ratio of ingredients). Way of blowing, adding food dyes, amount of food dyes, size of bubble blower and type of bubble blower	Length of time bubble lasts, size of bubble, number of colours seen, Observation and ranking	Year 5 or 6	Conclusions as letters to companies producing washing liquid has provided some good responses

Table 5.2 *Continued*

Investigation context and global questions	Independent variables	Dependent variable	Year group	Notes
Sc 2 How to get the cleanest teeth?	Type of tooth paste, amount of tooth paste Type of mouthwash, amount of mouthwash Types of apples, fruit and veg, amount of, time spent chewing, Chewing gum Teeth sticks	Amount of plaque seen with disclosing tablets – percentage, fractions or arbitrary scale	Year 5 as the maths is difficult and a survey of teeth is best suited to Year 3. This is a survey rather than a fair test although the groups can fair test each different aspect.	Gain permission from parents prior to activity. Watch member of class who might want to investigate what happened to amount of plaque over time (is not cleaning teeth at all for days!)
Sc4 Which is the strongest magnet?	Type of magnet, size of magnet, materials	Number of layers of paper/materials effect occurs through. Number of paper clips picked up, height off ground that paperclips attached, distance across table	Year 3	A range of different ways to ensure the effect. The work should focus upon the results and method rather than explaining what magnetism is and how it works (domains) so patterns and trends are expected outcome
Sc4 Which spinner will stay in the air for the longest time?	Type of material, size of spinner, adding paperclips, height of drop, wholes in wing, number of holes, length of wing, width of wing, structure of blade, way it is dropped, height of drop, etc	Time taken to fall, number of spins, observation and ranking	Year 6 as possibilities are unending and it makes a good investigation to practice skills	Provide a template for pupils to vary one factor otherwise this is a DT activity and no trends and ideas can be developed as a class. It is vital that how it is dropped is looked at because the answer is to do with surface area not mass. Also if the spinner is made to take account of rotation it will stay in the air longer.
Sc4 What factors will change the brightness of the bulbs?	Type of bulb, number of bulbs, voltage of batteries, length of wire, thickness of wire, etc	Brightness of bulb, whether it lights or not		Be careful with varying length as copper wire will only be noticeable with a light sensor. If length of wire is to be changed use high resistance wire which will change over 1 m
Sc4 Which burglar alarm with two switches would be most effective at keeping a house safe?	Different types of switches, problem solving. Circuit needs to be made and two switches selected and introduced to circuit	Whether the switches work when tripped.	Year 4	This is not a fair test investigation and is problem solving.
Sc 2 What changes take place over time?	Type of plant, type of animal location	Measurements of change, size, colour etc.	All years possible but focus and type of plant and animal should be changed	Not a fair test and a survey throughout the year. Emphasis is on taking measurements and keeping a diary of the changes

Table 5.2 *Continued*

▶

Investigation context and global questions	Independent variables	Dependant variable	Year group	Notes
Sc 2 What factors affect the speed of germination?	Range of seeds, range of germination conditions, light, water, heat	Time taken to germinate Percentage germination	Year 5	Parsley will take months, change the size of the seeds to enable the pupils to check out a range of types. When germinated grow on till end of life cycle to demonstrate that seeds produce plants that produce flowers and more seeds (outside)
Sc 2 What factors affect the growth of plants? (Y6) or Where do most plants grow? (Y2)	Type of plant, type of area, size of area	Number of plants, tally of one plant observation and ranking	Year 2 and Year 6 – different outcomes and locations	H&S taking children out of classroom. Use a metal coat hanger as a quadrate
Sc 2 Which year group has the greatest visits from the Tooth Fairy?	Age of children	Number of children	Year 3	Survey across a school collecting data and storing year to year
Sc3 What makes balls roll furthest?	Type of ball, size of ball, type of surface, height of drop, way of letting go	Distance travelled in cm or using string/coloured wool. Comparison and ranking	Year 4	String can be used to help with pupils who have problems with graphs – hold up length and it becomes a graph. This activity needs a lot of space but balls can be replaced with marbles

Table 5.2 *Continued*

Summary

Procedural understanding involves all the processes used when investigating an idea. It represents the ways scientists work. These skills need to be taught to pupils but pupils also need to have opportunities to undertake the process of investigating an idea themselves, going through all the stages of scientific enquiry. A framework was presented to help with continuity and progression throughout the primary age range. Some suggestions for different investigations were provided, with both the global question and some possible variables identified. These investigations were not just of the fair test variety. As scientists tackle different questions in different ways, so pupils need opportunities to carry out 'a fair test', surveys, sorting and comparisons, problem-solving and to investigate changes over time.

CHAPTER 6

Planning and Assessing Learning

Hellen Ward

Introduction

Assessment is all the processes used to plan lessons appropriately and to evaluate them to enable pupils to learn to the best of their ability. It is not just about recording and reporting. This chapter will explore the whole area of assessing science in the primary classroom.

Assessing Children's Learning in Science

There are only three ways of gaining evidence about how pupils are learning: by observation, discussion or marking/looking at completed tasks. Unrealistic expectations affect assessment in science because it is not possible to listen to every conversation or to observe every child in every situation, and a focus only on the completed task is limiting. Choices have to be made about how assessment information is collected and used. Involving other adults is helpful but involving the pupils is essential. In science, observation is vital. Through observing pupils working, judgements can be made about their ability to use equipment, their co-operation, creativity and perseverance. By observing how a pupil undertakes tasks, information about current and future learning needs is provided. Discussion with and between pupils is essential as it provides information about their ideas and thought processes. It also provides important insights into ways of working, and information about the concepts and processes the pupils are using. A programme over time for observing, and speaking with, all pupils should be planned. However, in reality it is mainly completed tasks that teachers assess through marking: the write-up, drawings and diagrams, or responses to test questions. This will not provide the 'full picture' of the processes and learning that have taken place. It is therefore important to use a mix of all three approaches, but also to understand that each has advantages and disadvantages. For example, with older pupils, assessing completed tasks can provide reasonable information, whilst with younger children, those for whom English is an additional language or those with special educational needs, the assessment of written tasks will provide limited insight, particularly about processes of learning.

Assessment for Learning

The Assessment Reform Group (ARG, 1999) defined the terms 'assessment for learning' and 'assessment of learning'. Assessment for learning is the formative processes used to develop children's learning; the knowledge of where children are at a given time and the skills of enabling them to progress to where they need to be. Assessment of learning is often considered as national, or end of unit tests but it can be any method that judges learning at a given time.

The introduction of national testing in England and the annual publication of school results have led to judgements that link quality of teaching to test outcomes. As always when such links are made, and this phenomenon has been observed in many countries, teachers adapt their approach and 'teach to the test'. A direct outcome is that areas not tested become 'less important' and there is more emphasis on teaching strategies to 'pass the test'. An example within science teaching was the suffix 'er' 'rule', for descriptions, e.g. 'the high*er* the slope the furth*er* the distance'. This type of question, however, was not included in national tests in 2004. 'Teaching to the test' practice has started in Year 5, and in some schools throughout Key Stage 2. The focus upon assessment **of** learning has a negative impact upon teaching.

Assessment **for** learning starts with the long-term plan. Each school has its own ethos and identity, indeed this is encouraged through *Excellence and Enjoyment* (DfES, 2003). The long-term plan maps the appropriate experiences the school provides for pupils to gain the knowledge, understanding and to acquire the skills outlined in the national documents from Foundation Stage to the end of Key Stage 2. It should indicate the time allowed for each subject but also make clear where links between subjects provide for more realistic experiences in learning. National schemes do not reflect local or individual school contexts and, as a result, many schools, particularly at Key Stage 1, are beginning to plan science that matches their needs (OfSTED/HMI, 2004). This is a positive move.

Planning for Assessment

In medium-term plans, specific learning objectives, opportunities for meeting them, the resources required and assessment strategies are detailed. In many schools this will be the QCA/DfEE (1998) scheme of work (Figure 6.1), or a similar published document. Although not statutory, such a scheme reduces the need for teachers to make decisions about time and content to ensure the needs of pupils are met.

Science is about knowledge and understanding, but is also about progression in acquiring skills and developing procedures. A medium-term plan outlines progression in all areas of science from Year R through to Year 6. Using the plan to track an 'imaginary' pupil as they move through the school, it is possible to plot the science the pupil would experience and to identify areas of learning that occur regularly and aspects not covered so often. Through work with science co-ordinators, it is apparent that many pupils are exposed to a great deal of repetition. Using 'food and healthy eating' as an example, lack of progress occurs when 'a healthy meal' is repeatedly the focus for learning. Although science teaching is cyclical and aspects are repeated, the learning must be developed and this is unlikely to be achieved by revisiting the same activity again and again.

This lack of progression is found with many other units. Problems occur when repeated experiences have no development whilst clear planning ensures pupils' experiences and opportunities are developed and motivation is encouraged. National schemes may help with planning for progression, but they need to be reviewed critically. It is important each school only uses a scheme as a starting point. Just because a scheme has a 'seal of an expert' does not mean it is perfect for every school. In QCA/DfEE (1998) science scheme, sound is covered in Year 1 and not again until Year 5. However, the pupils' answers given in national tests and discussed in the annual standards report, indicates that pupils' understanding of sound is not well developed. In part this underdevelopment of aspects of sound might be linked to an overall lack of music teaching. The Office for Standards in Education and HMI (2004) acknowledges that a curriculum focusing mainly upon numeracy and literacy will affect other areas of learning. This illustrates why schools need to identify appropriate links in the curriculum that enrich learning and meet the needs of its pupils. Breadth and balance are also important but in the QCA/DfEE scheme there are many more units that focus on Life and living processes (Sc2) compared to units on Materials and their properties (Sc3), or Physical processes (Sc4).

Year group	Learning intentions	Activities	Types of recording	Types of outcomes
Year 1	■ That **we need to eat and drink to stay alive** ■ To record their ideas about food using drawings and charts	■ Discuss with children their ideas about why we eat and drink	■ Help them to record these in drawings or simple charts	■ That humans and other animals need food and drink to stay alive
Year 2	■ That humans **need water and food to stay alive** ■ To record information in drawings and charts	■ Find out why they know about the importance of drinking water and eating a variety of foods to stay healthy	■ Help children to make a record of the groups	■ State that if we don't eat and drink we will die
Year 3	■ That all animals including humans, need to feed ■ That an **adequate and varied diet is needed to keep healthy**	■ Visit a local supermarket or market to look at the range of foods available or use secondary sources and a collection of foods. Group foods into broad categories ■ Present children with a collection of pictures to illustrate types of food from different cultures	■ Ask children to record their groupings in drawing and writing ■ Ask children to describe using drawings and writing how they aim to have a balanced and varied diet	■ Produce a record of the visit or work done in writing and drawing ■ Describe a varied and balanced diet suggesting some foods that are needed for growth and some that enable us to be active
Year 5	■ That **to stay healthy we need an adequate and varied diet**	■ Help children to use secondary sources to find out about foods which are rich in fats/oils, those which are rich in sugars/starch and those which provide materials needed for growth	■ Help children to produce a display illustrating adequate and varied diets or a week's menu	■ Identify foods needed for growth and those which provide for activity

Figure 6.1 *Lack of Progression adapted from QCA/DftE (1988)*

After tracking learning across the school, it is important to look at the yearly slices focusing upon what pupils receive in each year. This is not only the responsibility of a science co-ordinator but also the class teacher. This level of scrutiny should focus upon the experience and opportunities for science. If science is only perceived as a body of knowledge, then the focus will be on subject knowledge learning intentions. The way lessons build upon each other also needs evaluation and also the time provided for pupils to develop their ideas and skills. One reason pupils give for not liking science is that they are not aware of links and progression in learning. 'Every lesson is different and there is no link to what we have done before', said a less literate boy in Year 5. The amount of unfinished work in books supports this 'stretch it thin' approach.

The development of skills (see Chapter 2), is an area gaining importance in science teaching, but if learning is going to be successful for all pupils, then understanding of, and working with, the level descriptions are essential. The learning and attainment of each cohort of pupils will vary but so will each pupil's progress in each aspect of science. These differences are not just in understanding but also experiences, expectations and enjoyment. Although the national expectation for most pupils in Year 2 is Level 2 and in Year 6 is Level 4 this is a broad-brush approach and teachers need to know what skills, processes and understanding are required to meet each level, and to plan with these in mind. By sharing an understanding of the elements of the level descriptions, in words they can understand, pupils can begin to recognise where they are and what they need to do to improve their learning.

Teaching and learning are often discussed together as though inextricably linked, however, just because teaching occurs learning is not guaranteed. Understanding of the progression of skills enables the different needs of all the pupils in a particular age group to be met. This differentiation is vital and needs to occur in every lesson.

Case Study 6.1

In a Year 2 class studying materials and their properties, the expectation was initially set at Level 2, *making a number of observations*. However, within the class there were pupils who were not working at this level. The learning intention remained the same but the activity/outcome was altered slightly to enable pupils working at Level 1, *to observe and communicate in simple ways*, whilst more able pupils were expected be to make *more observations and some measurements*. The majority of the pupils were working at Level 2, so were expected to make comparisons. With 30 pupils in the class, basing all assessment of learning on observation or discussion only was impossible, so a mix of approaches was used. For most pupils the outcome was demonstrated as a completed task, which was a set of drawings with some words; for other pupils information was obtained through discussion. There was little opportunity for direct observation but questioning by the teacher occurred. The more able pupils were able to add measurements to their observations whilst less able pupils only drew one picture and were supported with writing. Planning totally different tasks for the range of abilities usually results in teachers supporting tasks and not teaching pupils – the juggling the balls and plate-spinning type of lesson – here all the pupils had the same basic activity. It was important to consider the challenge factor in this activity as pupils who are given low-level tasks and less interesting equipment can become bored and uninterested.

It will have struck some readers that the activity that the pupils were undertaking was not mentioned. This omission relates to the issue of activity rather than learning-driven science lessons. The activity could have been melting using the bags referred to in Chapter 9 (odd one out). If the activity is selected first then learning is reduced. It is important that pupils' ability in science is not confused with issues such as limited literacy skills. Only quality assessment will provide information on learning in science.

Her Majesty's Inspectorate (2004) reports progress in meeting the needs of less able children in science but that more is needed for the most able. In all classes the outcomes should be related to the level descriptions. This ensures that the pitch of many activities is not too low and pupils are required to demonstrate attainment at higher levels: sorting and grouping is Level 2 and explaining and use of scientific language is Level 4.

The Use of Level Descriptions in Planning

The level descriptions can also be used for planning for knowledge and understanding. There are two aspects to this, the first is the specific knowledge elements and the second concerns pupil understanding. If the programme of study is set out like a helix (Figure 6.2), it is noted that aspects occur at different levels. For example, although an understanding of whether things are living or not only occurs explicitly in a programme of study at Key Stage 1, it is actually identified by the level descriptions at Level 3. Therefore, teaching this only in Key Stage 1 and not in Key Stage 2 impacts on pupils' understanding.

The second way of using the level descriptions for understanding is to identify progress level by level across the programme of study. Using Sc2, Sc3 and Sc4 only and starting with Level 1, key words can be identified. For example, across all three aspects Level 1 is about communicating observations in oral and written form. The understanding needed at Level 2 is about sorting, grouping and classifying. Incidentally, this comparison element of Level 2 is also in history and

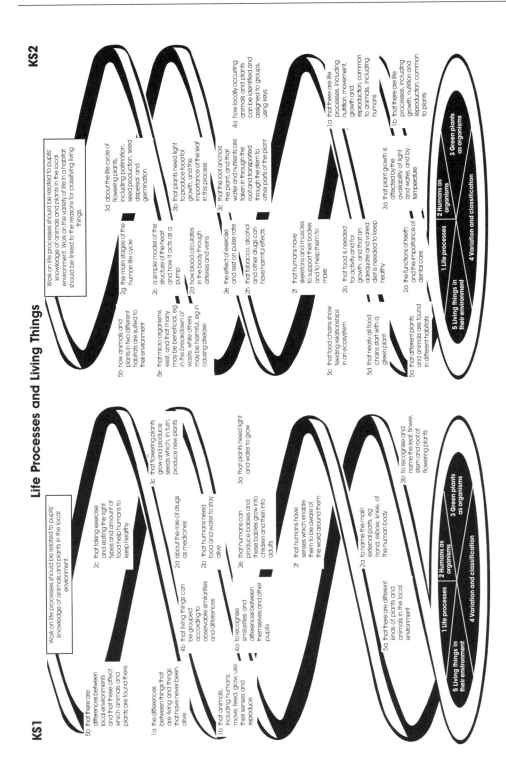

Figure 6.2 *Helix*

geography and allows further links between subjects. Level 3 can be classified; 'cause and effect', for example, overeating causes weight gain, rougher surfaces have greater friction. These simple generalisations are usually difficult for pupils at Key Stage 1 to understand.

Figure 6.3 demonstrates the progression at each level. This can be used to plan learning intentions, using the idea that 'if I know what I am looking for, I am more likely to spot it when it happens'. When used in this way the lesson has an appropriate pitch and the focus is on learning rather than activity.

Level	Knowledge expected
1	Communicate observations
2	Sort group, compare, similarities and differences
3	Cause and effect, simple generalisations and simple explanations
4	Explanations using scientific vocabulary. Generalisations
5	Abstract ideas and models

Figure 6.3 *Knowledge at different levels*

Case Study 6.2

The Year 2 pupils were still undertaking work on materials and their properties. The activity related to rocks. The knowledge requirement for the pupils was set according to Level 2, in line with national expectations. The learning intention shared with the pupils was *'to sort objects into groups and to make a simple record'*.

The success criteria was *'to be able to place all rocks in groups that share the same property and to be able to record them in these groups'*.

A few of the pupils were not yet at the level where they could sort and group and draw pictures, so they were given hoops in which to put their rocks and some support through questioning and discussion. Another group were beginning to sort, so they were given a small number of samples with very obvious properties. They had previously been supported with small hoops and vocabulary cards. Most of the rest of the class were sorting and grouping and drawing the results in their books. They exchanged ideas and used their own science dictionaries for appropriate words. The higher-achieving pupils explained their sorting using a greater number of rock samples, some of which required more than simple observation by sight. For this lesson there was no additional support but if there had been, then the lower ability group could be given opportunities to work with an adult, to extend their vocabulary, or one of the middle groups could have been questioned and challenged to give simple explanations for their groupings. Assessment was relatively easy because the learning intention and success criteria were clear and ▶

had been shared with pupils in language they understood and the majority of the learning was pitched at Level 2. Towards the end of the session the pupils evaluated their work, deciding if they had achieved the success criteria. Those that did drew a smiley face, if not then a sad face was drawn. The pupils were clear about the purpose of this, and assessed themselves well. It had taken some weeks to train them in this method. Some pupils drew a straight mouth on their face, as they were unsure. At the end of the lesson the books were reviewed. Some pupils were only able to draw the rocks and talk about them using science words provided by the teacher. They were not working at Level 2 and needed more support. Most pupils were able to compare and sort (they had met the learning intention) and a few pupils provided simple explanations. This demonstrated that they were working at a higher level. These assessments were fed directly into the next lesson.

Sharing Learning Intentions

Many teachers now plan lessons by identifying learning intentions. Often, however, there are too many learning intentions in a single lesson and this confuses both teacher and learner. Evidence demonstrates that sharing learning intentions is vital and that writing it on the board or displaying it in a prominent place is also important. These should be written in 'child speak' thus enabling pupils to talk about what they are going to learn and to think about how they will know they have learnt this. If learning intentions are not shared in this way, then the link between the learning of the lesson and the pupils' ability to self-assess is lost. Writing the learning intention on the board in Reception classrooms enables pupils to identify and talk about the learning in the lesson even though the pupils cannot read the words themselves. It does, however, contribute to them learning to read. Where the learning intention was only shared orally in a Year 2 class, even the literate able children were not sure what the lesson was about

When planning learning, Clarke (2003) stresses the importance of separating the learning intention from the context of the learning. In Case Study 6.3 the learning intention is, 'to sort objects into groups', and it is important pupils understand that they are learning to sort. The context in this case happens to be rocks, but it could be any other material. If this separation of intention and context is not clear, then, Clarke has found, the pupils become more focused on the rocks than sorting. In order to move learning forward it is important in planning to consider the following questions:

- What will this lesson look like when it is completed?

- Which pupil/s need(s) to be extended further?

- Which pupil or groups of pupils will need to be supported?

- Will non-teaching assistants, teachers or pupils provide the support?

- How will the pupils communicate their findings?

- Will a worksheet provide the outcome required?

Worksheets have some benefits but only when produced in-house to meet a specific purpose. However, many worksheets used to provide differentiation often contribute to lack of challenge and excitement in science lessons. Key issues teachers need to consider are the level of literacy of the materials, the type of words used and the density of text. Many commercially produced worksheets that can be photocopied promote science as a comprehension activity, a colouring sheet or 'flat work'. A 5-year-old pupil at the start of Year 1 coined this term. When asked about his view of learning he stated that it was better in Reception because in Year 1 it was all 'flat work'. On closer questioning it was revealed that in Reception opportunities were provided to build, explore and investigate but in Year 1 this was replaced by endless sheets of paper, 'flat work'! The cost to science budgets for worksheets is enormous, with some schools spending so much on photocopies that they have inadequate science resources. The cost to learning is priceless.

Evidence of achievement has been one of the difficult issues over the last decade and has contributed to poor practice. The use of worksheets can de-skill pupils, whilst encouraging pupils to do their own drawings, take photographs and construct tables produces considerable learning gains with the acquisition of science skills, enjoyment by pupils and a reduction in budget costs. When the same approach is introduced at Key Stage 2 the process is harder because pupils have lost their independence and it takes time to regain this or learn the skills. Initially, books are untidy but the end results are worthwhile both for teachers and pupils. Observations and discussion with pupils using worksheets demonstrated that the focus was on completing the sheet rather than learning. When one pupil is doing the work and the rest of the group copying, assessment is difficult. It is impossible to assess understanding with work copied off the board. The enjoyment and creativity of learning should not be stifled by the chore of recording, and this mechanistic approach will not enable self-assessment or feedback marking.

Grouping should be based on assessment of pupils' scientific knowledge, understanding and skills, and not on ability in any other subject. Grouping in science needs to vary according to the aspect being taught as attainment might vary across aspects. For example a 'less able' Year 1 child was able to lead the class session on electricity, as he knew what electricity was, where it came from and how it was created at a power station. This knowledge was as a result of out-of-school learning, and it helped that his father was an electrician! He was able to produce and understand electrical circuits, draw diagrams and communicate his understanding at a much higher level than the other pupils. The class teacher encouraged and developed his skills and as a result his self-esteem was raised.

Whenever learning is assessed a judgement is also being made on the quality of the teaching. At the end of a lesson reflect upon:

- the elements that were successful

- the level of pupil motivation

- the clarity of teacher explanations

- the effectiveness of resources

- the effectiveness of the activities.

These evaluations help to adjust the lesson next time this unit is taught as well as inform the next lesson in the series. It is important that the lessons in a unit are not set in concrete with the sole intention to get through them: pupils' progress and learning are the first priority. At the end of a lesson it can be helpful to record and evaluate the learning.

Figure 6.4 provides an example of a simple formative system. Up arrows demonstrate attainment above the expected (a more challenging task now needs to be set!), dots mean that these pupils achieved appropriately, and down arrows indicate pupils that did not meet the intentions (and therefore need further support). The next lesson should be amended in light of this and a series of assessments will provide information on attainment and indicate changes in overall performance for a particular pupil. For example, if a pupil who had been achieving highly starts to perform less well, this should be investigated. It could be the aspect of science that is a problem, or that they missed a lesson where a key skill was taught, or that there are issues at home. This type of assessment is only formative if it is acted upon by the teacher and/or pupil (Black and Wiliam, 1998).

Class Record Sheet – Year 5 Children Assessment Focus																	
Can describe the function of the heart, lungs and circulation system in the body																	
Can explain the link between increased heart rate, pulse rate and increased exercise																	
Can explain similarities between the life cycle of plants and humans																	
Knows that when we exercise muscle works harder																	
Can explain what a micro-organism is and some of their effects																	
Can explain that the differences in environmental factors affect the distribution of plants and animals in habitats																	
Can recognise and describe relationships using food chains																	
Knows that green plants make their own food																	
Can use scientific terms to describe changes																	
↕		 A															

Figure 6.4 *Simple formative system*

© 2005 Hellen Ward *Teaching Science in the Primary Classroom*

After each activity pupils should know if they have met the learning intention and be given opportunities for future action. Feedback marking and feed-forward planning needs to occur on a lesson-by-lesson basis until the very end of the unit of work, when a summative judgement is made. This should be recorded, as next half-term the work will be in a different aspect of science. The end-of-unit judgement will contribute to information about the pupil's progress over the year and will be reported to parents and other colleagues. If level descriptions are used to plan the learning intentions then the level a pupil is working at is known. Assessment for learning in science only works if pupils and teachers take action on learning needs. If books are marked with a comment of 'good': there is no action to take the learning forward as well as no indication about why it was good or if it was all good. Clarke (2001) stresses the importance of teachers and pupils understanding where a pupil is now and where they should be at the end of the unit of work, i.e. the gap in learning. Feedback through marking should enable the teacher to help the pupil 'close a gap'. In order to enable pupils to progress, minding this gap is key. Clear feedback on what is good and why it is good, as well as how and where the work can be made better, is needed. Examples of feedback marking are on the website (www.paulchapmanpublishing.co.uk\resources\ward.pdf). In science, symbol marking works very effectively. The symbols used should be discussed with the pupils.

Case Study 6.3

The school was a small village school and OfSTED inspectors had identified assessment in science as an issue. The children in Class 4 were a mixed ability group of 28 boys and girls aged 10 and 11 years. The topic for the half-term was materials and their properties, and the teacher was keen to trial feedback marking. The pupils chose smiley faces to be used where work was good and met the learning intention; this was unexpected because of their age but it was unanimous. It was also agreed that on any piece of work two smiley faces would be recorded. Providing three for some, two for others or only providing one would be the same as giving numbers out of 10 or grades, which is known to be de-motivational for all but the brightest pupils. A triangle was chosen to indicate where the piece of work could be improved. At the end of each lesson work was marked and areas for improvement highlighted. The children then used the first five minutes of the following science lesson to look at what had been judged as good and to act upon the area for improvement. This provided a clear link between lessons as well as a clear and calm start. Opportunities for the teacher to talk with individual children to provide additional support were also possible. The pupils liked the system and always acted upon the marking. There was a steady improvement in the work of pupils of all abilities. Interestingly, after four or five weeks one child's work began to deteriorate, and despite looking very thoroughly at a piece of work only one smiley face was given. At the beginning of the next lesson Darren complained he only had one smiley face. Darren was challenged to find, and justify, where another smiley face could be given. At the end of the lesson Darren pointed out that he had found it impossible to give another smiley face as there was nowhere that met the criteria. The quality of his work was discussed with him and as a result his work returned to the high quality and standard of which he was capable. Using two smiley faces proved a useful strategy, as did the use of prompts to the children. As these were not all different it was possible to group pupils who had similar aspects to work upon and to build this into planning for the next lesson. The pupils became more aware of work that was good and could see there were opportunities to improve. They enjoyed the personal feedback and focusing the assessment on the learning intention, and using symbol marking took less than an hour for all the books. On some occasions the prompt given to move the learning forward was actually related to the pupils' science target, for example, *the ability to see patterns and trends in graphs and graphical representation.*

Another effective assessment strategy in science is marking by questions. At the end of the lesson the teacher writes a question at the bottom of the work. The pupil is challenged to provide an answer at the beginning of the next lesson. Teachers using this approach found that they were providing similar questions for the different abilities of the pupils and began to keep a record or bank of questions they could use in the future. These questions were reviewed by the science co-ordinator and related to the level descriptions. This ensured all pupils, but particularly the more able pupils, were appropriately challenged. The pupils' responses to the questions were very positive and HMI in a follow-up inspection report commented favourably on this assessment feedback for the pupils. Pupils can also mark their own work and can effectively assess their own understanding prior to the teacher marking the work.

Case Study 6.4

In a Year 6 class where OfSTED had previously judged that in science the most able children were not sufficiently challenged, the pupils assessed their work at the end of the lesson using both traffic lights and smiley faces. They put a red dot if they felt they had not understood the learning intention and had not made progress towards it. They put an amber dot if they felt that they were getting there but were still a little unsure, and they put a green dot if they felt that they had met the learning intention and had understood the work. They also used a smiley face system to enable the teacher to judge their enjoyment of the session. ▶

The smiley face demonstrated that they had enjoyed the lesson, a sad face if they had not and a straight mouth on the face meant it was OK. What was significant was when the pupils recorded green yes I understand it, but alongside straight or sad faces. In discussion, pupils said the work was too easy and they had not enjoyed the activities. Occasionally they had found the work was challenging and recorded amber but also a smiley face because they had enjoyed the challenge within the activities.

Summative Judgements

Formative assessment is vital to help progress pupils' learning, however at some points in time a summative judgement is needed to report to others. In 1998, in one large local education authority (LEA), 18 per cent of the schools recorded no Level 3 attainment in science at Key Stage 1, while one school recorded 97 per cent of their children at this level. This variability in Key Stage 1 results for science across the country is well known. By sharing judgements within a school and then moderating these with colleague teachers in neighbouring schools agreement about levels can be reached. Now the pilot for Key Stage 1 assessment is statutory, pupils' work in science should become part of the national audit/moderation process and improve overall confidence in teacher assessment both within and outside education.

The QCA website and the Science DfES on www.standards.dfes.gov.uk\schemes3 provide some examples of work that has been assessed and levels awarded. This is a useful starting point for teachers in schools and for sharing investigative work. Levelling work and justifying why it is, for example, a Level 1, a Level 3 or a Level 5, enables professional judgement to be improved, and this can only be good for pupils' learning. Over the past seven years, working in many schools and classrooms carrying out demonstration lessons in investigative science, a major weakness observed is the lack of Level 5 work in investigative settings. Scrutinising many books has demonstrated considerable over-teaching of subject knowledge often to Level 6 and beyond but with limited development of skills and procedural understanding other than a focus on the fair test.

Recording Systems and Testing

Ongoing assessment recording systems, of up and down arrows, helps with future planning because it identifies individual and groups of pupils where the pitch of learning has to be adjusted. However, it is also important that teachers plan observation and discussion time with pupils. Having a simple way to record the outcome of these activities has challenged teachers. Post-it notes to mark places in pupils' work are used by many Foundation Stage teachers, however, these can fall off and get confused with other things, making them less useful. Self-adhesive address labels pre-printed with the pupil's name kept on a clipboard, enables notes to be made during lessons. The labels are then transferred directly to pupil's record. One advantage of this system is that it identifies pupils for whom no assessment has been recorded because their label remains on the sheet at the end of the week. These pupils are often those who pass attention because they are 'average', quiet or just clever at avoiding attention. Some teachers will still want a tick list, showing those pupils who can perform certain tasks or who know certain things. Ticks need to be evaluated, judged, and hopefully, acted upon to ensure appropriate learning for pupils and, at the end of the unit of work, used to enable a summative judgement to be made. Decisions need to made as to whether these tick lists need to be passed to colleagues and will they want/use them? A card system that is accessible to teachers or teaching assistants is useful. There is a card for each pupil, stored alphabetically. As a lesson proceeds the appropriate card can be taken and comments with a date added. Similarly, systems that allow pupils to consider and record their own achievements are very successful. Pupils have sheets with statements to colour or tick when they are ready. The sheet contains statements such as 'I can use a thermometer', 'I can measure accurately' or 'I know what gravitational attraction is'. Teachers also use colour-coded plans: red for not known/covered; yellow for some understanding; and green for clear understanding. Recording takes time and is only worthwhile if the judgements are used to inform future planning. This is especially true when there is regular testing of pupils and scores are recorded: 'What do they mean?'

Testing is a worrying feature because so much science time is being used on such activities and rarely do teachers discuss responses with pupils to help extend learning. The *Post Note* report (POST, 2003) suggested that national testing and the resulting impact of 'teaching to the test' may be one of the features of children's disaffection and lack of enjoyment of science. In addition there is no evidence that testing improves children's understanding (ARG, 2002). Analysing tests and looking at whether questions are answered correctly or not will provide some information about aspects that might be improved by adjusting teaching and learning. Such changes usually only benefit the next cohort of pupils because those taking the tests have moved on. Teachers could use outcomes of tests more beneficially by spending time post-test discussing with pupils the decisions they made and how they would respond if asked a similar question in the future. Here everyone benefits from sharing ideas.

Evaluation

Whatever systems are in place they need evaluating. Planning and pitching lessons is vital and yet it is recording the outcomes that is often the focus of attention. This is counterproductive and focuses upon systems not pupils. A system that enables judgements to be made and moderated across a school but that has flexibility in the collection and collation arrangements is desired. Teachers should be able to use a range of methods that suits them and benefits pupils, such as information technology (IT), tick sheets, observations, card systems or traffic lights. It is more important that the assessment information is used and shared with pupils than teachers complete imposed tick sheets. Common reporting formats are needed to enable the summative judgements to be transferred (Figure 6.5).

Summary

Assessment comprises a number of processes and starts with planning. The long-term experiences need to relate to the pupils' needs, and repetition of learning needs to be removed. Challenging pupils to improve by pitching lessons appropriately and involving them in the process is essential. Pupils need to understand the learning intentions and be involved in the whole process, as learning is not something that can be done to others. Learning needs to be thought out in advance, each lesson building upon the last and opportunities provided to learn and not only to complete. Feedback should highlight success but also guide for the future, and summative judgements should be made in a way that is consistent and meaningful so that in the next year learning continues seamlessly.

Pupil record sheet									
Pupil name						**D.o.B**			
Yr	Sc1	level	Sc2	level	Sc3	level	Sc4	level	Comment
R		W 1 2 3		W 1 2 3		W 1 2 3		W 1 2 3	
1		W 1 2 3		W 1 2 3		W 1 2 3		W 1 2 3	
2		W 1 2 3 4		W 1 2 3 4		W 1 2 3 4		W 1 2 3 4	
TA									

Figure 6.5 *Suggested whole school record sheet*

Pupil record sheet

Pupil name   **D.o.B**

Yr	Sc1	level	Sc2	level	Sc3	level	Sc4	level	Comment
3		1 2 3 4		1 2 3 4		1 2 3 4		1 2 3 4		
4		1 2 3 4		1 2 3 4		1 2 3 4		1 2 3 4		
5		1 2 3 4 5		1 2 3 4 5		1 2 3 4 5		1 2 3 4 5		
6		1 2 3 4 5		1 2 3 4 5		1 2 3 4 5		1 2 3 4 5		
TA									
Test									

Figure 6.5 *Continued*

Key:
R – Reception, 1 – Year 1, 2 – Year 2, 3 – Year 3, 4 – Year 4, 5 – Year 5, 6 – Year 6,
TA – Teacher Assessment, Test – National Test Level

CHAPTER 7

Science from Stories

Claire Hewlett

Introduction

Stories, both true and imaginary, can offer a rich source of learning opportunities for pupils of all ages. The traditional folk tale, myths and legends and modern stories that deal with the world in which people live can all be used as a stimulus for supporting learning across a range of curriculum subjects including scientific investigation, as well as provide an everyday starting point for science. This chapter considers why stories should be used as a resource and how fiction can be used to develop scientific understanding, with a particular emphasis on the 7 to 11 age range (Key Stage 2). A range of practical investigations are suggested as a starting point to illustrate how scientific investigation might be linked to a selection of popular children's literature.

Why Use Fiction?

Fiction, which also includes poetry, provides pupils with opportunities to make connections between scientific concepts and their own life experiences by providing a frame of reference on which to base their learning. Stories provide a vehicle to link previously learnt concepts with new ideas. Good stories have the potential to motivate pupils by making them feel involved through the linking of their own understanding of the world to the characters within the book.

With new initiatives in teaching being encouraged, such as the proposals outlined within the Department for Education and Skills *Excellence and Enjoyment* (DfES, 2003) documentation, teachers are being expected to consider ever more creative ways of delivering the curriculum. Established research has shown that people learn in different ways and for different reasons, and using fiction as a teaching resource enables the teacher to encourage and support a range of different learning styles. It could also be argued that teachers who consciously plan lessons or topics around the use of stories are more likely to adopt a range of different teaching styles themselves in order to meet the needs of the class. The stories chosen in this chapter provide examples of how to interpret the curriculum in different ways in order to provide pupils with a stimulating and varied range of lessons that will involve them in their own learning.

Teachers involved in teaching Key Stage 1 regularly use stories both as a starting point and as a stimulus for teaching a range of curriculum subjects, including science. An impressive range of texts, often beautifully and imaginatively illustrated, that explore the world of the child are widely available. Texts such as *The Hungry Caterpillar* by Eric Carle, or *The Enormous Turnip* by Alexi Tolstoy are standard texts found in the book-corners of many infant classrooms, and pupils have opportunities to enjoy these stories on many levels.

This good practice tends largely to disappear in the Key Stage 2 classroom where teachers are less likely to utilise fiction as a resource within their science teaching. There are possibly several reasons for this; stories are longer and more complex so finding a story that suits a particular teaching need may be difficult. For the same reason it may be problematic to find a story that appeals to all the pupils in the class, or one which allows for continuity and progression within a topic area. With pressure on teachers to deliver a broad and balanced curriculum, teachers may feel there is not the time to spend reading a story as well as completing a scheme of work, that getting too involved in the story might result in losing the science. However, as the science content at Key Stage 2 becomes more abstract some of these ideas can be far removed from pupils' own experiences and understanding. Providing a context that pupils can relate to can help to make the learning more meaningful.

There are obvious solutions. It is not always necessary to read a complete text. Initially a story could be retold in a summarised form to provide the overall context, with relevant chapters then selected to provide the stimulus for further investigation. Another possibility would be to use a text that that has been read before that the pupils are familiar with, perhaps from another lesson, literacy being the obvious example. Also, it is not always necessary to be tied by the constraints of age-appropriate texts. Many picture books aimed at the younger reader introduce scientific ideas very simply but the underlying concepts are, in fact, quite complex and therefore the material is also relevant for older pupils. For example, a story such as *Mommy Laid an Egg* by Babette Cole introduces the concept of reproduction in an accessible way to younger children but could also be used for teaching about life processes at the 7 to 11 age range. One of the characteristics of stories for this younger age range is that they are often very humorous, and this can be an added advantage when teaching older pupils, helping them to feel more at ease when discussing issues they may feel embarrassed or worried about.

When thinking about what text might be suitable, it is important to be aware that fiction can be used in different ways and for different purposes. Think about the intention. It may be that the aim is to draw out the pupil's interest in a story to stimulate and develop lines of enquiry to do with a particular area of study, e.g. electricity or forces. Alternately, the aim could be to encourage the pupils to solve scientific problems within the story setting that certain characters have encountered, for example 'can we make a bridge to help the Three Billy Goats Gruff cross the river?' The story may come first with the science developing from it, or vice versa with the science prompting the selection of a relevant text. Some stories may lend themselves to a range of ways they can be used while others are very specific. A text such as *Danny the Champion of the World* by Roald Dahl provides plenty of opportunity for problem-solving activities to be undertaken in the classroom while also lending itself to supporting more particular areas of study such as the study of materials or forces. *Old Bear* by Jane Hissey, on the other hand, tends to focus on one thing and therefore could be used specifically as a starting point for an investigation, in this case looking at parachutes.

Developing Science from Stories

Whichever story is chosen, and for whatever reason, it is important to remember not to get overly involved in the text and carried away. Research has found that teachers plan for far more than they ever teach, make sure it is clear how the story is to be used and how it will be integrated into the science teaching. Think about how progression and continuity will be planned for. Read the story and decide whether it covers concepts, skills or attitudes. Then read the story, or the relevant part of the story, with the pupils and explore their areas of interest. From these initial 'idea showers' decide upon the investigations and focus upon particular targets.

The following points should help when focusing on planning:

- What exactly will the pupils be doing?
- How will they be doing it?

- Why do it? (What skills, concepts or attitudes are you hoping to develop?)
- Is the activity appropriate? (Matching needs, abilities, previous learning)
- What organisation will be needed?
- What resources, materials, equipment will be needed?
- Safety awareness?

Selecting Stories for Starting Science

The following stories illustrate how texts can be used to support the teaching of science by providing interesting starting points for investigative science. Many of the activities are aimed at Key Stage 2 in order to demonstrate how abstract concepts might be supported, but many of the activities, and indeed the texts themselves, could be adapted for pupils younger than this.

Stig of the Dump by Clive King

Published by Puffin (1963) ISBN number 0140364501

This modern classic about a cave boy transported into the modern world encompasses many areas of the science curriculum including the overarching requirements of the nature of scientific ideas. This story has great potential for investigating concepts within the science curriculum and also for developing cross-curricular links to other subjects, in particular design technology, art and music. The suggestions included here address several areas of the programmes of study so this story could be used to teach any one of these.

Materials and their properties

> *He crawled through the rough grass and peered over. The sides of the pit were white chalk, with lines of flint poking out like bones in places. At the top was crumbly brown earth and the roots of the trees that grew on the edge. Some of the trees hung over the edge, holding on desperately by a few roots ... Barney wished he was at the bottom of the pit . And the ground gave way. (pp. 2–3)*

Taken as a stimulus for work on materials, a suitable starting point might be studying rocks and soils, then moving on to looking at changing and separating materials. Activities could include:

- Starting with some careful observational work, adopt a rock or pebble. Memorise the characteristics of the pebble by observation of the size, shape, mass, texture, colour. Can pupils identify their own rock when all the rocks are grouped together? Rocks and soils can be investigated further by testing the hardness of different rocks – scratch test – and testing for permeability. Can the pupils devise their own investigations to do this?

- What is soil? Can the class make soil? Design and make a wormery (DT links). Pupils could consider how Stig might filter his drinking water.

- Changing materials can be investigated by undertaking activities such as making fossils. Use plasticine to make casts from shells, fossils or leaves then pour in a plaster of paris mix. This activity could be a starting point for investigating reversible and non-reversible changes.

- Look at pictures of cave paintings, is it possible to produce rock paintings using different soils or by extracting colour from fruit or vegetables? Consider how charcoal is made, drawing with chalk and charcoal.

Forces and motion

The slab of rock was lying flat on the ground. Twelve men with pointed stakes pushed them under the edge of the rock and levered it about a foot off the ground ... The men with the poles and ropes made ready again. This time it was different: because of the steepness of the slope they couldn't pull from the front, but had to do all the lifting and pushing from behind. (pp. 152–4)

This section really lends itself to the investigation of forces, in particular studying pulling, lifting and exploring concepts such as friction and gravity. There is great potential for problem-solving here by presenting pupils with some open-ended questions that relate to the characters in the story and that provide opportunities for a wide range of investigative work, for example:

- What happens when more stones have to be pulled up a slope?

- What happens to the force needed as the mass increases?

- What happens when the slope is steeper?

- Where would most force be needed if moving a stone up a slope, the front or behind?

■ Which surface makes moving the stones easiest?

■ What is the best way to lift or lever a stone off the ground?

This sort of questioning encourages pupils to plan fair test investigations and think about how they will record their results in a systematic manner (a planning format would work very well here). Practical work on pulling and lifting, using stones, containers, slopes, different surface materials and Newton meters, will help to develop conceptual understanding of friction and gravity. Pupils could start by investigating what happens when the weight of the stones in a container is increased when the container is pulled along a flat surface. Are there any patterns in their results, what can they conclude? Pupils could then progress to investigate the effect of slopes by pulling a fixed mass up different gradients. Can they first predict what might happen? Can they explain their reasoning? Still using the same basic equipment, they could move on to explore the concept of friction and look at how different surfaces affect the pulling force.

Although using levers and pivots is not a requirement of the National Curriculum for science in the junior school, this type of investigation does allow for work on gravity and friction to be extended further and is well within the capabilities of upper junior pupils. How might a very simple lever mechanism help to move a stone or help stand a stone upright? A simple way of demonstrating this principle is by using a wooden ruler balanced over a pencil, like a see saw, and placing a heavy object on one end. By exerting pressure with a finger on the other end pupils can explore what happens when the pencil, or fulcrum, is moved nearer to or further away from finger or object. The story ends with the characters at Stonehenge, pupils could then develop their ideas further to investigate how they might move or lift stones to create a small-scale Stonehenge in the school grounds.

Light and sound: the Earth and beyond

and over the shoulder of the downs appeared a red spark, and the valley was flooded with light. It was sunrise. From the low mist in the bottom of the valley appeared the spire of a church, the tops of oast houses and electricity pylons. (p. 156)

This part of the story provides an opportunity to tie this work in with Earth and beyond, particularly looking at day and night, or as a stimulus for exploring the concept of light. Their small-scale model of Stonehenge could be used to investigate shadow formation and they could track the movement of the sun during a school day and look at how shadows can be used to tell the time.

The Iron Man by Ted Hughes

Published by Faber and Faber ISBN number 9780571141494

Materials and their properties: physical processes – electricity, forces and motion

This dramatic story lends itself in particular to topic work on electricity and magnetism, and the exploration of metallic materials and their properties:

> *The gulls took off and glided down low over the great iron head that was now moving slowly out through the swell. The eyes blazed red, level with the wave-tops, till a big wave covered them and foam spouted over the top of the head. The head still moved out under water. The eyes and the head appeared for a moment in a hollow of the swell. Now the eyes were green. (pp. 17–18)*

The links to metal and magnetic properties tie this activity into science in every-day life. Pupils could begin by exploring the properties of different metals and considering the different uses of metals. They could then test different metals for their magnetic qualities and record their findings in simple charts or tables. Questions such as 'Are metals with magnetic properties still attracted to mag-nets through different materials such as card, water or fabric?' could be answered. Get the pupils to plan different ways of testing the strength of a range of magnets. Is strength related to size? Results could be recorded in a variety of charts or tables devised by the pupils on the computer.

What would be the best metal for the Iron Man to have been made of? What happens to iron when exposed to salt water? Technically looking at rusting is no longer in the National Curriculum but it could be included as part of the breadth of study requirements and it does provide opportunities for pupils to plan their own fair test investigations if they explore what makes nails rust. Rusting is a major economic cost to the industrialised world. Is it possible to prevent rusting? Here would be a good opportunity to place primary school sci-ence within the bigger picture.

Stories can often give rise to misconceptions regarding scientific concepts, as the need for dramatic effect often takes precedence over scientific fact. During this story the Iron Man's rusty exterior turns back to shiny rust free metal. Is this possible in the manner in which it is told? These kinds of misrepresenta-tions in stories could be the basis of investigative work and used to challenge pupils' knowledge and understanding. Pupils can try to solve the problem of the characters either from the Iron Man's point of view or that of the villagers.

The changing colours of the Iron Man's eyes are referred to several times throughout the story. Besides looking at how to construct simple circuits and switches pupils always find experimenting with flashing light bulbs in circuits fascinating. What makes the bulb flash? What will happen to another bulb in a series circuit when a flashing bulb is included? Again open-ended questioning can be used to get the pupils exploring for themselves and coming up with hypotheses about the flow of electricity around a circuit. Make either a two-dimensional or three-dimensional model of the Iron Man's head, or look further at robots and make a whole iron man from construction kits or from suitable materials. Can the pupils make a model where the eyes flash different colours or flash on and off for a fixed period of time? Can they make the eyes flash alternately or alter the brightness of the eyes? Upper Key Stage 2 pupils, could investigate simple variable resistors in order to do this.

Dr Dog by Babette Cole

Published by Sagebrush Educational Resources ISBN number 0613845218

Life processes and living things

This book, aimed at the 4 to 8 age range, uses a medical pretext to indulge the reader in a range of outrageous scatalogical jokes. As with many of her other books there is some serious teaching underpinning the humourous and some-what ridiculous storyline, in this instance the dangers of smoking and unhealthy eating and the importance of washing hands to prevent spreading germs. Again, it is a story that could be enjoyed by pupils in Key Stage 2 as well as by younger pupils. This is a fun resource to support the teaching of life processes and to reinforce the concept that all living things need to undertake several processes in order to live. Pupils are often confused about life processes and what this involves, even at the end of Key Stage 2, and stories can help to make these more explicit when studying either plants or animals.

The dangers of smoking is part of the Key Stage 2 programme on drug awareness. The effect of smoking on the lungs could link to other work on life processes, in particular the importance of exercise and the role of the lungs within the circulatory system, and there are plenty of opportunities for practical work, for example comparing lung capacity. Comparison questions such as 'Do taller pupils have a bigger lung capacity?' could be investigated. Further comparisons could be investigated such as 'Do pupils with longer legs jump further, run faster?' and so on.

Grandpa's rather distasteful eating habits could provide a starting point for work on nutrition and the need for a healthy and varied diet. Pupils can survey what their classmates bring in their lunch boxes, keep a food diary, plan a healthy meal for the Grandpa character in the story. How the body can be affected by poor diet could be explored through looking at the function and care of teeth or, again, linked to work on health and fitness. Investigate how much hidden sugar is in someone's daily diet by reading the ingredients on packaging. With older juniors, studying packaging can be a helpful way of learning about micro-organisms. More universal issues could be considered such as how poor diet affects children in other countries.

Understanding the digestive system is not a requirement in the curriculum for the 7 to 11 age range, however, pupils are often fascinated by the journey of their food through the body and have no problems with understanding the processes involved if taught to their own level. Taking basic scientific information as a stimulus for creative writing, or just as a means to record what has been learnt, can be very productive. The digestive process is an exciting story in its own right and lends itself to imaginative 'adventure' story writing (Figure 7.1). Getting pupils to write their own science stories and poems provides

Figure 7.1 *The digestive process*

opportunities for self-expression and provides an interesting diversion from the more formal formats often used when writing up a science investigation. (See Chapter 5 page 68). The digestion story also makes a useful starting point for drama and could be used as the basis for a role-play drama and presented to other pupils. Posters and health warnings can also be used to convert the findings of an investigation and be displayed in the classroom or around the school. These are particularly effective when used to support work on life processes, for example personal hygiene to prevent the spreading of germs, or healthy diet to promote growth, healthy teeth and bones.

Tables 7.1 and 7.2 provide some further suggestions for how fiction might be used as a starting point for science when exploring the environment or looking at forces based on a topic on flight. Both figures include many activities or investigations that can be adapted across the 5 to 11 age range, though some are specifically targeted at an appropriate age range. The stories selected represent a very small sample of the wide range of fiction available to support science teaching. Texts aimed at the 5 to 8 age range are also generally suited to the teaching of concepts with older junior-aged pupils.

Summary

This chapter has considered how fiction can be used as a vehicle to support learning in science. By linking previously learnt concepts with new ideas, fiction can provide a frame of reference on which to base future learning. Fiction provides opportunities for making connections between scientific concepts and their own life experiences. Making only small changes to existing planning and practice, to include more use of a wide range of fiction, can enable teachers actively to promote pupils' creativity and respond to their creative ideas and actions. Fiction is a powerful and readily available resource to support and engage pupils with their own scientific understanding. Good stories have the potential to motivate pupils by involving them through linking their own understanding of the world to the characters within the book. Specific examples from well-known children's literature have been presented to illustrate ways in which fiction might be used as a science resource to support a range of teaching and learning styles. Further suggestions for development are included in Tables 7.1 and 7.2. The chapter has also briefly explored how pupils might develop their own self-expression through writing about their science understanding in a variety of ways.

Over the Steamy Swamp by Paul Geraghty	Superb illustrations that bring to life the world of a swamp.
Tadpoles Promise by Jeanne Willis and Tony Ross	Embodies life cyles of frogs and butterflies as a tadpole and a caterpillar fall in love with dire consequences
The Tiny Seed by Eric Carle	One of several books by this well known author that teaches about life processes.
Diary of a Worm by Doreen Cronin	Hilarious retelling of a worm's life from his own perspective.
Our Field by Berlie Doherty and Robin Bell Corfield	Three children make an exciting discovery in their summer holidays.
The Secret Garden by Frances Hodgson Burnett	A secret garden, walled, locked and forgotten. Can it be brought back to life? A children's classic.

Careful observation of the environment. Take young children on nature walks and mini safaris to look for things, e.g. flowers with 3/4/5/6 petals, plants that match colours on a paint palate, leaves with different textures, shapes etc. Trees are plants but are often left out of the curriculum – adopt a tree, what lives in your tree, how tall is your tree, measure the girth with non standard measurements, how does it change throughout the year?
Cross-sections or transects of a chosen area enable children to observe very carefully what is living in different areas, e.g. under a tree, by a path, near a hedge in the middle of the field? Again suitable for 5 to 7 age range, older children can record random sampling using hoops or ropes to mark a small area, what is living within? What conclusions can be drawn?

Classify plants and animals by their different features by recording observations in table form. The 7 to 9 age range can identify locally occurring plants and animals and assign to groups using simple keys, older juniors can make their own. Grow plants – beans in jam jars against blotting paper allows children to see the root system develop, suitable for a range of ages particularly 7 to 9-year-olds. Devise a database.

Pond dipping – find out about life cycles of insects. What lives in the bottom, middle, on the surface of the pond? Use keys to classify different insects. What type of plants live in a pond, at the edge of a pond? Look at interdependence between plants and animals. Compare the habitat of the pond with another area around the school.

Design a small wildlife area for your school, what conditions could you provide for plants and animals? Consider the life processes, what is necessary for plants and animals to survive. Undertake a survey to establish living conditions of snails, woodlice or earthworms. Use secondary sources to answer questions that arise when observing living things. Design a home for some woodlice so they can be kept in the classroom.

Children in the nine to eleven age range can **identify simple food chains in an ecosystem**. Food chain game – children get to be something (e.g. sun, grass, cow, man) and have to put themselves in order. Record food intact from yesterday. All food comes from plants or animals, find out where your food comes from to develop simple food chains (links with geography). Write a dramatic food chain story or act it out as a drama.

Older juniors can explore **food webs and develop the concept of food chains**, some animals eat different things eg herons will eat other things besides fish. Use secondary sources to develop ideas about ecosystems, contrast food webs from Britain with webs from other habitats/ecosystems (*Over the Steamy Swamp*, though aimed at the 5 to 7 age range is an excellent resource for older pupils). Link children together with string to show these complex links. Look at a food chain starting with a mosquito and ending with man, what are the implications? What happens when disease wipes out something in the food chain?

Table 7.1 *Further suggestions for use of fiction as a starting point in science*

Old Bear by Jane Hissey	Old bear has been stored in the attic, can his toy friends think of a way of getting him down?
Flat Stanley by Jeff Brown	Stanley Lambchop awakes one day to find he has been flattened. Various adventures follow including being flown like a kite.
The Eagle and the Wren by Jane Goodall	A tale about flight and how a tiny wren outwits a mighty eagle.
Danny Champion of the World by Roald Dahl	Much loved tale about a boy and the relationship he has with his father. Making a hot air balloon and flying kites are included in two chapters
The Blue Between the Clouds by Stephen Wunderli	A novel about a friendship between two boys and their mutual passion for flight.

Many of these activities can be adapted for children of different ages:

Drop a weight from different heights into a sand tray. Predict what will happen first. Will there be any difference to the depth of the imprint? What will happen if the height of the drop is altered? Younger children could investigate this and observe what happens, older junior age children could hypothesise before testing.

Drop a screwed up ball of paper and a flat piece of paper from the same height, what happens? What happens if two similar size containers are dropped from the same height simultaneously, one empty and one filled with plasticine?

Drop items that are made out of the same materials but are different shapes, what happens? Predict which will fall the slowest and give reasons why?

Make kites, paper planes, spinners or parachutes. Investigate which stay in the air the longest, travel the furthest, are the most aerodynamic etc. (adapt the following investigations). Again, younger children could observe what happens whilst older juniors can develop their own investigations by raising their own questions, identifying variables, thinking about how they might record their results. Explore questions such as:

Parachutes:

- Are some materials better than others for making parachutes?
- Why does a parachute come down slowly?
- What happens if there is a hole in the centre?
- What happens with more than one hole, which is the best number of holes, does the size of the hole make a difference?

Spinners:

- Investigate the factors that keep a spinner in the air for the longest time. What can be changed, measured, recorded? For example, number of wings, length, shape, material. Do they fly better when weighted?
- Look for patterns in results.
  Draw pictures showing the direction of the forces with arrows.
  Look at birds and how they soar on thermals.
  Look for photographs of early attempts at flight and compare some of the factors to those discovered in a paper airplane contest.

Links with mathematics; find out how much fuel an aeroplane consumes, work out how much is consumed on set journeys.

Table 7.2 *Further suggestions as a starting point for use of section 2 in science*

CHAPTER 8

Using Role-play to Stimulate and Develop Children's Understanding of Scientific Concepts

Julie Foreman

Introduction

This chapter will include a brief overview of the theory underlying the use of the whole body, in kinaesthetic experiences, to promote pupils' learning in science. Role-play will then be explored as a kinaesthetic tool to promote primary school pupils' understanding of abstract scientific concepts. Throughout the chapter the importance of teachers modelling this approach will be emphasised along with the importance of providing opportunities for pupils to practise role-play as a valuable tool of learning. Incorporating role-play with relevant talk will ensure that pupils' understanding is developed effectively. Practical suggestions for work in the classroom will follow. Finally, to raise awareness and to avoid misrepresentation, the limitations of the use of role-play will be highlighted.

Teaching Approaches in the National Curriculum

The National Curriculum (DfEE, 1999, p.83) encourages teachers to adopt a flexible approach to teaching science when it states that pupils should be taught 'that science is about thinking creatively to try to explain how living and non living things work'. Therefore, pupils should be encouraged to use their imagination and develop their creativity in science lessons. This view is echoed in the more recent *Excellence and Enjoyment: A strategy for primary schools* (DfES, 2003) and is particularly important throughout the primary years.

Some would argue that imagination, rather than knowing facts is the most important factor needed to learn science and, therefore, the use of imagination should be reflected in its teaching. Without doubt, science is an integral part of modern culture and must aim to stretch the imagination and creativity of young people. The ability to think creatively is an essential attribute of the successful scientist. Therefore pupils should be given the opportunity to respond to aspects of science in an imaginative and a creative way. This is especially important if it is to nurture future scientists, since both creativity and an ability to communicate ideas clearly to others are two important characteristics of successful scientists.

The implications of this for primary science teaching are huge. Recent OfSTED reports have highlighted that teachers must challenge pupils of all abilities, particularly the most able, much further than at present, and that pupils need to experience more complex forms of learning. After all, it is generally accepted that pupils can achieve more if they are challenged in a non-threatening, motivating way.

Whilst it might be that traditional approaches to teaching science may not stifle creativity in some pupils, it is well known that many people have been put off science in the past by their own experience of science in school. However, it is easy to accept that the development of an individual's creativity in science may well be dependent upon the quality and diversity of the learning opportunities provided in the classroom. In fact, it has been found that if too few opportunities are provided for pupils to show curiosity then their motivation to engage in creative behaviour can easily be dampened. So, it is important to approach activities in a creative way ensuring that risk and exploration are encouraged.

Writers on the subject believe that the brain thrives on diversity, so there is a need for the provision of diverse teaching and learning strategies. Pupils learn in different ways all the time, and there is no one 'right' way for all. Therefore teachers need to draw upon a variety of different approaches in their teaching to cater for the variety of pupils' learning styles.

Research tells us that that active learning approaches such as role-play, which engage the intellect in enjoyable, less threatening ways, should play a much larger part in science education than it has in the past. The self-perpetuating saying 'I hear and I forget; I see and I remember; I do and I understand', shows the importance of practical activities. Role-play is one such practical, creative experiential teaching technique (Van Ments, 1983, pp.14–23). Research findings indicate that role-play, as a form of physical modelling, can help pupils to visualise and understand abstract scientific concepts. Here, understanding comes not only through participants' high level of involvement, but also through exposure to ideas, discussion and collaboration with other learners.

Role-play has been shown to build upon pupils' natural enjoyment of play and can provide much fun and real interest. Role-play can be considered to be a very natural learning medium when one considers how much time very young children engage in undirected, imaginative, fantasy play both in their own play outside school and, when given the opportunity, in the nursery and Early Years classroom. This natural tendency to engage in role-play can be harnessed by the teacher in a more structured way to encourage learning about aspects of science. What is more, role-play is motivational because it involves activity and provides a break from established classroom routines.

Movement can represent or exemplify what cannot easily be put into words (Bruner and Hasle, 1993 p.169). Therefore, since role-play involves physical movement, it can be used to help to explain abstract concepts. Recent research into how the brain helps to construct learning suggests that movement is potentially an effective teaching strategy in developing lifelong networks of connections in the brain (Smith, 1999, p.33). Here, the human body is considered to be a 'powerful route into learning' (Smith, 1999, p.178). This form of physical learning can be termed as a kinaesthetic learning style, viewed as a 'bodily-kinaesthetic intelligence' by Gardner (1993, p.9). However, role-play demands more than just bodily movement. There is also a need for interaction and collaboration. In this way, the needs of a range of learning styles can be met. Role-play can also be viewed as a valuable learning experience which integrates different areas of the brain (Smith, 1999, p.37). Added to this notion, creative activities such as role-play allow pupils not only to communicate using familiar language codes, but may encourage pupils to communicate using 'language usually restricted to scientists' (Taylor, 1997, p.39), thereby developing their use of scientific vocabulary.

In order for role-play to be effective in giving an insight into a scientific way of thinking, it is important that the teacher models an idea before it is practised by the pupils. To achieve maximum benefit, role-play should be used regularly in science from the earliest days in formal education and throughout the school. In this way, pupils become familiar with this strategy and therefore will develop their confidence in participation – confidence being a powerful factor in learning. Familiarisation has been shown to develop pupils' ability to use role-play more effectively to show their learning and so provide a form of assessment of their learning. The use of role-play has also been shown to illustrate abstract scientific concepts and to facilitate pupils' retention of the knowledge gained.

Role Play in the Primary School

As stated above, it is important that role-play is incorporated into school schemes of work so that pupils can become familiar with this teaching strategy and confident in participation. Role-play is already an important strategy in the early years of schooling, though not necessarily for the development of scientific knowledge and understanding. It is very common for very young children in school to 'act-out', for example, an extract from books of traditional tales and to engage in more informal role-play in the 'home corner'. It is easy, therefore, to extend this idea to simple scientific ideas at the Foundation Stage. It is easy to link literacy to science in this way. The use of 'props' is important in role-play. Older pupils will benefit from the use of labels and pictures during the delivery of their role-play. Younger pupils may well 'dress-up', wear masks or dress models to help to communicate scientific ideas.

One difficult concept for younger children to understand relates to forces, i.e. pushes and pulls. Here, following the reading of *The Enormous Turnip*, small groups of pupils can role-play parts of the story to pull the enormous turnip from the ground. In doing so, their understanding of forces will be developed. Similarly, many scientific concepts can be explored through role-play starting with a story, or observation. Older pupils can often approach the representation of ideas in a very creative, imaginative way if they are given the opportunity to put forward their own ideas after brief instruction.

Table 8.1 illustrates how other topics can be developed through the use of role-play throughout the school. However, it is important to appreciate that many of the same ideas can be approached at different ages and abilities. Here, it is the role of the teacher to choose the level of the idea to be explored and to decide how much help to give to pupils in formulating the role-play. For example, within the topic of electricity, whilst younger pupils may only be asked to represent the flow of electricity in an electric circuit using a skipping rope, older pupils could be expected to role-play, e.g., the flow of the electrons, the pupils themselves acting as the electrons in a circuit. Concepts such as resistance, series and parallel circuits could then be developed in this way.

Topic	Age group	Aspects of role-play
Shoes (Scientific aspect: Materials and their properties)	Foundation Stage	Pupils think about the properties of the materials used for different kinds of footware, e.g. soft warm fabric for slippers, stiff leather for boots and some shoes, flexible materials for beach 'flip-flops' and 'jelly' shoes. Pupils then to act out one of these to demonstrate the properties.
Mini-beasts	Foundation Stage	Following observation of mini-beasts, pupils could pretend to move like different creatures: props could include, e.g. additional limbs to enable pupils to become spiders or insects. A small sleeping bag can make a good 'prop' for the skin of a caterpillar.
Waterproofing	5–6 years	Ideas related to the properties of materials: some materials can let through water others cannot. Pupils enacting the particles of water and different materials.
Day and night	5–6 years	Ideas relating to the movement of the Earth in relation to the Moon and the Sun. Pupils enacting the spin of the Earth in relation to the Sun to show how day and night occur.
Electricity	6–7 years	Push the push: pupils to stand in a circle holding a rope and pass it through their hands to illustrate the flow of electricity. One pupil could act as the light bulb and slow the movement of the rope.
Shadows	7–8 years	Ideas related to how light travels: Some materials allow light to pass through whilst others do not i.e. exploring opaque, translucent and transparent materials. Pupils enacting the path of the light and how it may be reflected, passed through or absorbed by the material in its path.
Thermal insulation	8–9 years	Ideas related to heat transfer: Why ice cream does not melt when wrapped in newspaper and why newspaper keeps chips hot. Pupils representing the heat transfer and the newspaper, i.e. the heat is prevented from passing through the newspaper either from the outside, or the inside of the package.
Dissolving	9–10 years	Ideas about solubility: that some things will dissolve in a liquid, whilst others will not. That there is a limit to the amount of substance that will dissolve in a liquid. Pupils acting as the particles of a liquid and the material to be dissolved.

Table 8.1 *Aspects of role-play that could develop from different starting points*

▶

Topic	Age group	Aspects of role-play
Filtering	9–10 years	Ideas about particle size: that some particles are too big to pass through a filter, whilst others are not. Some pupils acting as the filter letting some particles through, other pupils acting as the particles trying to get through the filter.
Evaporation	9–10 years	Ideas about movement of particles: puddles evaporating. Pupils acting as the particles of a liquid changing to a gas – without boiling.
Sun, Moon and Stars	9–10 years	Ideas relating to the position and movement of planets around the Sun.
Sun, Moon and Earth	10–11 years	Ideas relating to the position and movement of the Earth around the Sun and the Moon around the Earth. Pupils to act as the Sun, Earth and Moon to show the orbits of the Earth and Moon. The same side of the Moon facing its orbit can be enacted and the length of one complete spin of the Earth explained.
Food webs	10–11 years	Pupils acting as the Sun, plants and animals in a number of food chains using string to link them appropriately. Cross-link food chains to show a food web with the Sun at the centre.
Sexual reproduction in plants: pollination	10–11 years	Pupils can take the role of the sex organs of flowering plants such as the stamens and the stigma. One pupil then acts as a pollinator (e.g. a bee) flying from flower to flower.
Making a classification key	10–11 years	All pupils in the class to line up and discuss/develop questions with yes/no answers to group/classify the pupils as in a branching key, e.g. Does the child have blue eyes?
Heart and circulation	10–11 years	See Case Study 8.1.

Table 8.1 *Continued*

Case Study: From Role-Play to Drama

This case study comes from a three-form entry primary school situated in the centre of a small town in the South East of England. The class contained a wide range of abilities with a high proportion of pupils with special educational needs. Pupils in Year 5 had been undertaking a topic on health and fitness, including learning about the circulatory system. The teacher realised than many pupils in the class were confused about this process and she felt that the diagrams in the available non-fiction books were difficult to interpret by many in the class. The teacher decided to involve the pupils in a role-play as a way to develop their understanding of the circulatory system. The role-play consisted of the journey of the blood between the lungs and heart. This was used to explain how oxygen and carbon dioxide are transferred to the organs of the body by the blood.

The school, like many others, had a tradition of each class taking turns, each week, to present a class assembly which parents were invited to attend. The class in question, when it was their turn, decided that they would like to present their role-play from earlier in the term. The class were accustomed to making their own decisions about what and how to present their assemblies, so, after initial discussion, the class were left alone to plan for themselves. What resulted was an extended version of their original role-play into a scripted drama that included actions, expressions and dialogue. The narrator, electing to wear a white laboratory coat, goggles and a red wig, and armed with a clipboard and pointing stick, proceeded to act out the role of 'mad scientist'. Whilst explaining the journey of the blood around the body, some of the pupils were organs strategically placed around the hall, whilst the remainder of the pupils took the role of the corpuscles. The corpuscles moved around the hall filling up with oxygen in the lungs and slowly running out of oxygen as they moved around the body feeding the organs.

When the class were preparing their 'leavers' service the following year they were asked to write about their favourite memories. The narrator wrote about their play and could still recall the main teaching points he had learned the year before.

The Use of Role-Play in Two Areas of the National Curriculum

The remainder of this chapter will look at the use of role-play in two areas of the curriculum based upon work with a class of Year 5 pupils, i.e:

- solids, liquids and gases

- sound.

In each example, the National Curriculum references covered by the role-play within the Programmes of Study will be highlighted. Guidance will be provided to show how role-play can be used to physically model these scientific concepts. Photographs will be included for illustration. Suggestions will be made for points to emphasise during the role-play in order to challenge pupils' possible misconceptions. Additionally, this section will outline possible group extension activities to enable pupils to use role-play to show their conceptual understanding. Finally, this section will present examples of possible outcomes of using these approaches in the primary science classroom.

It is important, before undertaking any role-play activities, that the issue of scale in relation to pupils acting as the particles is clearly explained to them as we are dealing here with a highly abstract concept.

Solids, Liquids and Gases

What follows are specific suggestions for how pupils can be organised to undertake the role-play.

Making a solid

What are you trying to show?

Solids, liquids and gases form part of Sc3 within the National Curriculum, i.e. Materials and their properties. It is expected that 7–11-year-old pupils should be taught to recognise differences between solids, liquids and gases, in terms of ease of flow and maintenance of shape and volume.

Pupils are to represent particles (atoms and molecules) in the role-play.

Teaching points

■ The particles in a solid can only vibrate in fixed positions, they cannot move around because the particles are tightly bound – ask the pupils to simulate this by wobbling.
■ The solid has a fixed shape and volume. It cannot change its shape only when another force is applied – this can also be simulated.

What do you need?

Examples of solids for pupils to examine their properties. Pupils could also bring into school, lists of solids investigated at home, or on the Internet.

How do you prepare the class?

Pupils to investigate a range of solids and establish the properties of a solid.

Running the role-play

Select nine pupils to form a solid. Arrange them in rows of three and ask them to link arms as shown in Figure 8.1.

Questions to use

Before the role play:

If we were to become the particles in a solid (explanation of scale would be needed here), how could we show the properties of a solid?

During the role play:

How can we show that the particles in a solid can only vibrate in fixed positions and cannot move around?

How can we show that the particles are tightly bound and a solid has a fixed shape and volume?

After the role play:

Discussion to reinforce the properties of a solid referring to the role-play.

Follow-up work

Pupils to record the properties of a solid referring to the role play using a method of their choice, such as:

- cartoon strip
- newspaper article
- poster
- diagram
- story in the life of a solid
- poem.

Further role-plays on liquids, gases and change of state to be covered next.

Figure 8.1 *Photograph of pupils role-playing a solid*

Making a liquid

What are you trying to show?

Solids. liquids and gases form part of Sc3 within the National Curriculum, i.e. Materials and their properties. This states that at Key Stage 2 pupils should be taught to recognise differences between solids, liquids and gases, in terms of ease of flow and maintenance of shape and volume.

Pupils are to represent particles (atoms and molecules) in the role-play.

Teaching points

- The particles are still closely bonded but they can 'slide' around in each other in a liquid.
- Liquids can change their shape to fit the container they are in – this can be simulated by 'pouring' the liquid particles into a contained area made by tables or chairs for example as shown in the photograph.
- Liquids keep the same volume when they are poured from one container to another. The liquid particles could be 'poured' into another arrangement of chairs but the number of particles remains the same.

What do you need?

Examples of liquids. Pupils could bring lists of liquids from investigation at home, on the Internet, etc.

How do you prepare the class?

Pupils to investigate a range of liquids to establish the properties of a liquid.

Running the role-play

Select another nine pupils to make a solid again and explain that you are a source of heat to be applied to the solid.

In a solid that will melt, the particles begin to vibrate/wobble faster and they gradually become a liquid when a temperature is reached that causes the particles to vibrate/wobble so fast that they break free of their bonds and begin to flow.

Ask the pupils to 'drop' their linking arms and 'slide' around each other as shown in the photograph in Figure 8.2.

Questions to ask

Before the role play:

How can we change a solid to a liquid?
How does a liquid differ from a solid?
If we were to become the particles in a liquid, how could we show the properties of a liquid?

During the role play:

How can we show that particles in a liquid are still closely bonded, but can slide around each other?

How can we show that liquids can change their shape to fit the container they are in, but keep the same volume?

After the role play:

Discussion to reinforce the properties of a liquid referring to the role-play. Further comparison of the properties of a solid and liquid.

Follow-up work

Pupils to record the properties of a liquid referring to the role play using a method of their choice such as:

- cartoon strip of how a solid changes to a liquid
- story to describe the journey of a liquid
- flow diagram of what happens to the particles in a solid as it changes to a liquid
- poster to compare the properties of a solid and a liquid
- diary in the life of a solid and how it changes to a liquid.

Further role-plays on gases and changes of state to be covered next.

Figure 8.2 *Photograph of pupils role-playing a liquid*

Making a gas

What are you trying to show?

Solids, liquids and gases form part of Sc3 within the National Curriculum, i.e. Materials and their properties. This states that at Key Stage 2 pupils should be taught to recognise differences between solids, liquids and gases, in terms of ease of flow and maintenance of shape and volume, and also about reversible changes, including dissolving, melting, boiling, condensing, freezing and evaporating.

Pupils are to represent particles (atoms and molecules) in the role-play.

Teaching points

■ Gases have no fixed shape or volume and they can spread out to fill any space or container – the pupils running around to the extremities of the room space can show this.
■ The particles are spread out with nothing between them, moving fast and in all directions – the pupils as particles may occasionally bump into each other and change direction to simulate the gas.
■ The particles of a gas can be squeezed into a smaller space – pupils moving from the playground space to the classroom for example can simulate this.
■ Warming a gas makes its particles move even faster and further apart, causing them to press harder on the sides of a container or space.

What do you need?

Examples of gases. Pupils could bring lists of gases, from investigation at home, from the Internet, etc.

How do you prepare the class?

Pupils to observe and discuss where gases are found to establish the properties of gases.

Running the role-play

Select another nine pupils to make a solid, then a liquid, by warming the solid as before.

This time by adding more heat the particles move around each other more easily until they move so quickly that they escape from the surface of the liquid.

Ask the pupils to move very quickly around each other and then one by one leave the 'liquid' and move quickly in random directions around the room space as shown in Figure 8.3.

Questions to ask

Before the role play:

How can we change a solid to a liquid, to a gas?
How does a gas differ from a solid and a liquid?
If we were to become the particles in a gas, how could we show the properties of a gas?

During the role play:

How can we show that particles of a gas can spread out to fill any space or container and have no fixed shape or volume?
How can we show that particles of gas move very fast and in all directions?
How can we show that the particles move even faster when warmed?
How can we show that particles of a gas can be squeezed into a smaller space?

After the role play:

Ask questions to elicit from the pupils what they have learned about the properties of a gas – referring to the role-play in order to reinforce the concepts.
Further comparison of the properties of a solid, liquid and gas.

Follow-up work

Pupils to record the properties of a gas referring to the role play using a method of their choice such as:

■ cartoon strip of how a solid changes to a liquid to a gas
■ story of life as a gas particle
■ poster showing a range of gases in everyday life incorporating the properties
■ newspaper article of what happens when a solid changes to a liquid to a gas.

Further role-plays, changes of state in everyday life to be covered next.

Figure 8.3 *Photograph of students role-playing a gas*

Possible group extension activities to enable pupils to use role-play to show their conceptual understanding.

After these illustrative role-play activities pupils can be grouped to show through role-play the concepts (in Table 8.2) for assessment purposes and to provide opportunities for presentation and whole-class discussion to clarify any arising misconceptions:

Possible role-plays	Links to National Curriculum	Instructions on how this can be managed
Evaporation What happens to the water particles in wet hair as a hair dryer is drying it?	■ Materials and their properties ■ Changing materials ■ Reversible changes ■ The water cycle	Establish with the pupils the change of state taking place
Evaporation What happens to water particles when water evaporates from a puddle?	■ Materials and their properties ■ Changing materials ■ Reversible changes ■ The water cycle	Consider the motion of the particles in each state of matter
Condensation What happens to water vapour in the air as it hits a cold glass of water?	■ Materials and their properties ■ Changing materials ■ Reversible changes ■ The water cycle	Ask pupils what happens in the change of state in question – refer to the previously explored role-plays
Melting What happens when chocolate melts?	■ Materials and their properties ■ Changing materials ■ Reversible changes	Identify in chosen groups who is to act as one of the particles, who is to be the narrator and any other props, e.g. the hairdryer
Freezing What happens to water in an ice cube tray placed in the freezer?	■ Materials and their properties ■ Changing materials ■ Reversible changes	Groups of pupils then prepare their identified change of state role-play for presentation to the rest of the class
Boiling What happens to a pan of water as it is boiled on the cooker hob?	■ Materials and their properties ■ Changing materials ■ Reversible changes	

Table 8.2 *How to manage role-plays*

Note: It is important to make clear that most substances contract when they change from a liquid to a solid with the exception of water, which expands when it freezes. The pupils could be challenged to show this in the freezing role-play. Pupils could show this when they form the solid in the role-play by holding hands and pushing outwards rather than linking arms to show the bonds as in the previous examples.

Outcomes of using these approaches in the primary science classroom

Knowledge and understanding that matter is made up of particles and their arrangement and movement in solids, liquids and gases is not identified in the Key Stage 2 National Curriculum (DfEE, 1999, p.87) – this concept is identified at a level 6 understanding in Key Stage 3 (DfEE, 1999, p.23), although modelling is identified at level 5. However, research has shown that pupils at early secondary age show very little appreciation of the intrinsic motion of particles (Johnson, 1999, p.93). Other research has shown that pupils modelling the intrinsic motion of particles can enhance their understanding of the properties of solids, liquids and gases (Foreman, 2002 p.61). Below are some of the responses of a Year 5 class interviewed after taking part in the role-play of solids, liquids and gases:

I think when I look at solids, liquids and gases I will think of what is going on inside them. (Boy aged 9 years)

I learned that molecules actually move round, before I didn't know I thought they just stayed still and then if you move them and then they move. (Boy aged 10 years)

Because we got to do what they (particles) were doing and if you had to write it down you wouldn't know what they would be doing and what it would be like to be them. (Girl aged 9 years)

The pupils' class teacher stated that the use of role-play:

Helped to explain concepts that are very hard to understand. I think that really took them that stage further and also consolidated what they already knew ... it stretched them to the limit of what they could assimilate.

These pupils were also able to retain the knowledge and understanding attained through the role-play, when questioned at the end of the school year, with responses as follows:

We went into groups and showed how solids, liquids and gases move and we were the molecules. When the molecules were tightly bonded they were a solid, when they were free and filled all the space they were a gas and when they slide over and around each together they were a liquid. (Girl aged 10 years)

My group's role-play was when you had washed your hair and you are drying it with the hairdryer. The water started off as a liquid and finished as a gas because the hair was dried. We moved slowly at first but got faster as the hair dried. (Girl aged 10 years)

We could actually do what we felt but when you are writing you can't really do it ... Sometimes I find it hard to put my ideas down. It made it clearer than just normal speaking, cause we could actually do it and it would make us understand more. (Boy aged 9 years)

Sound

What are you trying to show?

Sound features in Sc4 of the National Curriculum, i.e. Physical processes. Here pupils should be taught that sounds are made when objects vibrate but that vibrations are not always directly visible. Also they should be taught how to change the pitch and loudness of sounds produced by some vibrating objects and that vibrations from sound sources require a medium through which to travel to the ear.

Use of the role-play

Pupils need the experience of representing particles (atoms and molecules) in solids, liquids and gases prior to the role-play activities relating to sound travelling.

Teaching points

- Sound can travel faster through solids than liquids and faster through liquids than gases.
- It is the sound wave that moves through the material/medium and not the particles of the material.
- The sound source vibrates and so vibrates the particles of the surrounding materials in the same way and this is how sound travels.
- Sound can only travel through materials, so cannot travel through outer space.

What do you need?

String telephones
Wooden broom handles
Plastic tanks filled with water
Inflated balloons

How do you prepare the class?

Pupils should investigate and observe how sound travels through different materials and states of matter (solids, liquids and gases).

Pupils can share observations about their experiences of sound travelling in the swimming pool, bath at home, etc.

Sound travelling through a string telephone

Divide the class in half, so that the pupils have the experience of enacting and 'feeling' the role-play and also observing the role-play. Arrange them in a single row with arms placed on the shoulders of the pupil in front, as shown in Figure 8.4. The pupils need to hold on tightly. Ensure that both halves of the class have both experiences and discuss their observations after the role-play.

Figure 8.4 *Photograph of pupils role-playing aspects of sound*

You will act as the sound source vibrating, rocking backwards and forwards, so that when you grasp the shoulders of the pupil at the end of the line they rock backwards and forwards and in turn they rock the pupil in front of them and so on down the line.

Pupils will be able to 'feel' the sound wave move down the line, through themselves as particles, and the observing half of the class will be able to see the sound wave move along the particles of the 'string telephone'.

Loudness or amplitude

Using the same arrangement as before with the pupils as particles in a string telephone with their hands placed on the shoulders of the pupil in front, the pupils can show the range of loudness by the extent of how far they as particles move backwards and forwards.

- For very loud sounds they can rock backwards and forwards a long way.
- For very quiet sounds they move a little way forwards and backwards.

Teaching points

- Loudness is increased by the size of the vibrations (amplitude) of the sound source being increased, such as hitting a drum harder.

Pitch or frequency

Using the same arrangement as for loudness, the range of pitch can be shown by how quickly the pupils as particles move backwards and forwards.

- For very high-pitched sounds they move very quickly backwards and forwards.
- For very low-pitched sounds the pupils move more slowly backwards and forwards.

Teaching points

- Pitch or frequency is that rate at which the vibrations go backwards and forwards.
- Small or short vibrating points cause the vibrations to move quickly and so the sounds they produce are high pitched.
- Long or large vibrating points cause the vibrations to move more slowly and so the sounds they produce are low pitched.

Questions to use

Before the role play:

What is happening to the sound source to create the sound?
When sound travels through a material how does it travel?
What happens to the particles in the material?
What happens to the particles in a loud sound?
What happens to the particles in a quiet sound?
What happens to the particles in a low-pitched sound?
What happens to the particles in a high-pitched sound?
If we were to become a string telephone, how could we show what happens to the particles as sound travels through the string?

During the role play:

Can you feel the sound wave travelling through?
Can you see the sound wave travelling through?
What is happening to the particles in the string telephone as the sound travels?
How can you show a loud sound travelling through the string telephone?
How can you show a quiet sound travelling through the string telephone?
How can you show a high-pitched sound travelling through the string telephone?
How can you show a low-pitched sound travelling through the string telephone?

After the role play:

Referring to role play:

> Why do you think sound travels faster through a solid than a liquid?
> Why do you think sound travels faster through a liquid than a gas?

Follow-up work

Recap on how sound travels, loudness and pitch.

Possible group extension activities to enable pupils to use role-play to show their conceptual understanding

Challenge the pupils in smaller groups to show the movement of particles in the following concepts:

- A low-pitched, loud sound.
- A high-pitched, loud sound.
- A low-pitched, quiet sound.
- A high-pitched, quiet sound.

Sound travelling through different materials

The concept that sounds can travel faster through a solid, than a liquid, than a gas can also be role-played drawing upon the experiences of the role-plays covered so far. However it may be more beneficial to set this as a group challenge for the pupils.

Possible group extension activities to enable pupils to use role-play to show their conceptual understanding.

In groups pupils can be challenged to show and compare what happens when sound travels through solids, liquids and gases and to explain why sound travels more quickly through solids, than liquids than gases.

Pupils will need to draw upon their knowledge of the role-playing of solids, liquids and gases, and how sounds travels from a vibrating sound source of previous role-plays.

Outcomes of using these approaches in the primary science classroom

Almost all the pupils who were interviewed after being involved in the sound role-plays were able to 'feel' the sound wave moving, which they considered enhanced their learning. Comments made by the pupils included:

> *It is easier to remember how sound travels now in the role-play, easier than writing it down.* (Boy aged 9 years)

The observation of the role-play was also beneficial for those who could not 'feel' the sound wave moving in the role-play:

I couldn't really feel the sound wave moving along but I could see it when the others were in the line. (Boy aged 9 years)

Similar to the outcomes discussed earlier, it was also shown that pupils were able to retain the knowledge and understanding attained through the sound role-play, when questioned at the end of the school year, with responses as follows:

I learnt that when sound travelled through the molecules we moved backwards and forwards. We call that movement vibration. (Girl aged 9 years)

We lined up and put our hands on the person's shoulder in front of you and one person at the back pushed the person in front and everyone moved forwards and backwards and created a sound wave. (Girl aged 9 years)

When a loud sound hits the molecules they go backwards and forwards a long way. When a quiet sound hits it doesn't go backwards so far. (Girl aged 10 years)

During their associated presentations the following comment was made:

The tighter the bonds are linked, the faster the sound travels through. (Boy aged 9 years)

When questioned later on in the year the following expression was recorded:

Sound travels most quickly through a solid because the particles are so tightly packed together that the sound can go through a lot easier for them to bump into them and to let the sound travel through the particles. (Girl aged 10 years)

Summary

This chapter has considered why role-play is an important and appropriate teaching strategy for use in primary science and has explored a number of ideas for use in the classroom. The following provides a number of issues to think about and points of guidance to consider when planning to use role-play in the classroom:

Issues

■ Role-play and drama can provide a break from established classroom routines, something pupils enjoy.

- Role-play can provide a fun way to focus pupils on specific aspects of value in learning.

- The physical modelling as a form of kinaesthetic learning enables pupils to understand abstract concepts.

- Role-play is a form of learning, which is accessible by all learners irrespective of ability and learning style.
- Pupils are very aware of their own learning and are able to retain scientific concepts through the physical involvement.

Guidance

- Initially there is a need for the teacher to model and intervene to support pupils' development of independence, confidence and proficiency in using role-play as a tool to show understanding.

- Grouping pupils to devise their own role-plays to show conceptual understanding challenges them through cognitive conflict to develop thinking.

- Pupils prefer to use role-play as the method to show their understanding as opposed to writing it down.

- Presentation of the role-play can provide a class with an opportunity to consolidate their own learning and the teacher with an opportunity for assessment.

It is hoped that the examples of role-plays discussed within this chapter and the evidence presented will inspire you to use role-play across the science curriculum to illustrate scientific concepts. What is most important is to consider pupils' creativity in devising their own role-plays. Your pupils may never to cease to amaze you with their imagination and ingenuity!

CHAPTER 9

Science from Games

Hellen Ward

Introduction

Games can offer many opportunities for pupils to learn both the knowledge of science and its associated vocabulary in an interesting way. With a large number of pupils choosing science as their least liked subject, serious action is needed. Reasons given for pupils' lack of interest in science include the 'writing down' elements and the dominance of teacher talk, but the focus upon revision, the impact of the national tests and the lack of interesting fun things in the curriculum also play a part.

Overall, the crucial question to be answered, is to what extent is much current practice really meeting the needs of pupils and society? This question is especially pertinent in relation to those pupils who are potential scientists.

How Can the Use of Games Enrich the Primary Science Curriculum?

Playing games of different types provides learning opportunities in all subjects, not just science. Play is well known to be a powerful medium for learning throughout a person's life. However, the use of play is not an element of learning in some classrooms and interesting science lessons are not found everywhere. As argued in Chapter 8, play and its associated teaching strategies can be used effectively to enhance learning and provide the motivation and long-term development of positive attitudes towards science.

It is now accepted that there are different learning styles. What is less well known is how this information can be used at the planning stage for learning. In some schools, though, the incorporation of different learning styles has become central to the way of working and teachers consciously plan visual, auditory and kinaesthetic (VAK) activities. However, whilst 'brain gym' and VAK have become popular in some subjects, currently the overall impact upon science teaching is limited. The focus in other areas of the curriculum has been on identifying the learning styles of groups of pupils and then directing targeted activities to their preferred learning type. However, in the long term, this may not be the best strategy for pupils, as individuals need to develop a whole raft of ways of learning and, therefore, a variety of styles and approaches should be used in teaching for all learners (Kolb 1984).

The benefits of using play as a positive strategy in the classroom can be enormous. However, allowing pupils merely to play in order to make an interesting lesson, in itself, is not the answer. Play has to be planned for and managed. In order for play to be used productively, pupils must be attentive and on task, the games must be motivating and fun.

To increase positive participation, depending on the games chosen, an element of competition could be introduced. Having a reason or an audience for the activity can enhance motivation. Team games in science are more motivating for all learners particularly when the teams are made of pupils of mixed gender and ability. If the game is designed in a way that encourages pupils to improve on past performance then they will be keen to learn vocabulary or concepts and may not even think of it as 'work'. This type of play is a 'win-win' situation, where all pupils work together to improve the class time or score rather than one group winning at the expense of the rest of the class.

Games can also be good for helping pupils with the hard-to-learn facts such as the life cycle of plants and are a good way to bring up complex issues such as drugs or smoking.

Developing Scientific Language through Games: Links to Literacy

Language development is central to learning science, and games that help with this should be encouraged. Bingo, chain (or link) games and matching words and definitions are all easy, fun and enjoyable. Bingo and chain games (Figure 9.1) are most effective if played in mixed ability teams to begin with, rather than all pupils having their own cards. These activities can later be used as individual games when confidence and understanding of vocabulary are raised.

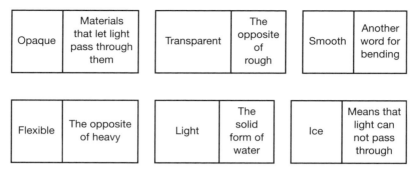

Figure 9.1 *Chain games*

Chain games start with one pupil or the teacher reading the first question, the answer being provided on a card somewhere else in the room. The person with the correct answer then reads their question and so the chain (or link) is made. It is important that the words used are discussed with the class since pupils may suggest more than one answer and the precision of word usage is one of the most difficult aspects of science for pupils to develop.

Subject-specific bingo (Figure 9.2), for example, on forces, helps pupils to be exposed to scientific vocabulary and promotes learning by immersion. Vocabulary development is always an area where pupils need help, and regular immersion for short periods of time is more beneficial to learning than exposure only once a week. Usually in bingo, gaining a 'full house' is the target, but here, because of time constraints, pupils could play just for one line. In this case, the teacher selects words according to the scientific topic under study and reads the definitions to the pupils. Although many games of this type are commer-

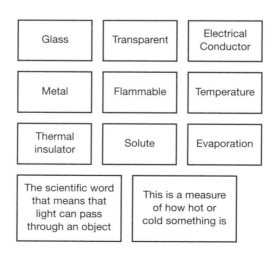

Figure 9.2 *Bingo*

cially produced, these can be made easily and cheaply using index cards. In this way, the game can be tailored to the needs of specific pupils and can make these ideas accessible to all.

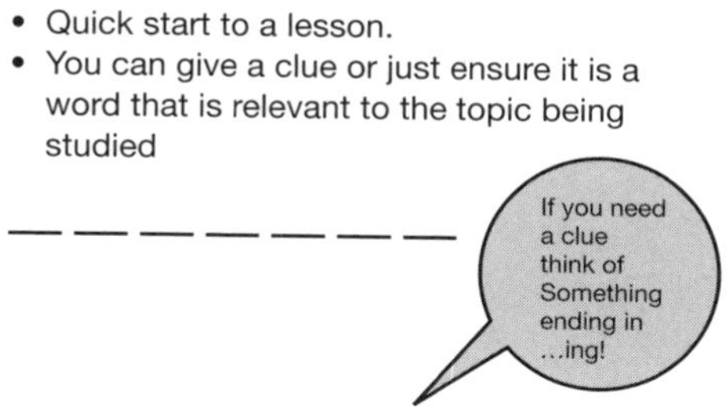

- Quick start to a lesson.
- You can give a clue or just ensure it is a word that is relevant to the topic being studied

_ _ _ _ _ _ _

If you need a clue think of Something ending in …ing!

Figure 9.3 *Hangman*

Scientific hangman (Figure 9.3) can develop pupils' visual vocabulary. When the word is guessed the pupils can gain extra marks from the teacher if they can define the term accurately. Here there is room for further discussion and exploration of the meaning of terms and so, in the long term, pupils will become more able to define terms accurately.

'I can think of three' is a quick and easy game to encourage pupils to use their thinking skills; for example, 'Name three solids that are opaque.' To increase the demand, older pupils in groups could be asked to think of as many opaque solids in three minutes. At the end of the time the group that has been able to think of the greatest number can be selected to share their ideas first. This enables common answers to be discussed. Other groups can then add any additional examples that the first group have not included. The debate and discussion that follows these activities are as important as the list generated. For example, a group of Year 6 pupils had a very lively debate on the state of matter of toothpaste as a result of the above challenge.

Crossword and word searches have always been used extensively in science, along with cloze procedures. When churned out in worksheet format the focus of the lesson can easily be lost and so can the fun. This does not have to be the case. If crosswords are produced on an overhead transparency (OHT) or on an interactive whiteboard, an effective lesson starter can be created. Pupils can then work together, for example, some groups solving the across clues whilst others focus upon the down clues. This is an easy way to introduce differentiation and helps pupils not only with the development of vocabulary, but also with the spelling of scientific words, i.e. if the words are spelt incorrectly they will not fit into the gaps.

Spelling of scientific vocabulary should be linked to literacy with older pupils and links should be made with the technical vocabulary requirements of literacy. The use of a small notebook for the collection of scientific words can be helpful. Better still, if this personal scientific dictionary is then carried by a pupil through a key stage it can become very useful for long-term reference.

The use of crosswords can be further developed by providing a completed crossword, but without clues. Pupils can then be challenged to produce the definitions. These definitions can then also be added to the pupils' own scientific dictionaries.

Starting from the answer and developing the question (Figure 9.4) provides pupils with the opportunity to think in more detail. For example, with the answer 'Space' there are many questions to which this word could be the answer, from 'Star Trek calls this the final frontier', to 'Sounds will not travel in this medium' and many more besides. Talking with pupils about the good questions, those that are truly questions, and those responses that are really definitions, is a skill that can be developed from this type of activity. Even teachers have found this to be a challenging activity. Removing the common term 'forces' from the centre box (Figure 9.4) provides a good starting point to enable pupils to link these ideas together.

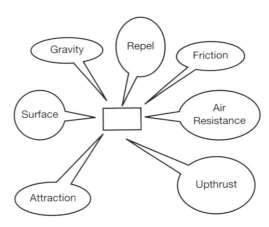

Can you give me a question for each of these answers?

Figure 9.4 *'What's the question?' challenge sheet*

All these ideas provide the opportunity for children to develop their communication skills and their ability to work co-operatively in a group whilst simultaneously developing their scientific knowledge and understanding.

The outcomes from this work can be linked to literacy lessons related to question raising. These activities can promote thinking by pupils and should be encouraged. Thinking skills can also be developed using the 'impossible question' idea; for example, 'What material cannot be washed?' Science and creativity go hand in hand and the teaching skills and ideas used today in primary schools could help pave the way for promoting and encouraging creative thinkers of the future.

Visual Memory Games

Using memory games can enhance visual memory and the ability to make links. The memory can be thought of as a muscle, i.e. the more that it is used the better it becomes. 'Kim's game' is a party game played by many children in the days prior to the video and computer age. Provide the pupils with a range of scientific equipment suitable for the topic being studied and allow the pupils to look at the selection for some time. Then remove the items from view and ask the children to name all the equipment that was provided and give its use. This causes discussions about the types of equipment as well as what they are used for. The development of observation skills is occurring as well as language skills; these functions are situated in different parts of the brain and are being made to work at the same time. Removing only one item could change this activity, requiring the pupils to identify what is missing.

'Talk about' cards (Figure 9.5) or posters help pupils with the difficult concepts that relate to their everyday lives. Providing the pupils with a range of statements and ideas about a topic, such as smoking or drugs, helps them to challenge the views given. Pupils should debate and evaluate the ideas on the card to refine their own views and opinions ensuring that they can provide

A cigarette contains about 4000 chemicals, many of which are poisonous. Some of the worst ones are: • Nicotine: a deadly poison • Arsenic: used in rat poison • Methane: a component of rocket fuel • Ammonia: found in floor cleaner • Cadmium: used in batteries	Smoking doesn't really help people lose weight. If that were true, every smoker would be thin. When people stop smoking they put on weight.
Smoking makes you smell bad, gives you wrinkles, stains your teeth, and gives you bad breath. Smoking makes people feel relaxed and makes them one of the crowd.	• Cigarette packages state that smoking kills. Do all people who smoke die? • Smoking a 'light' cigarette is a healthier choice.

Figure 9.5 *'Talk about smoking'*

evidence to support these views. This is a good starting point for fact and opinion work in other subjects and can stimulate the need to use research skills. It also allows some difficult topics to be discussed by pupils without it appearing that the teacher is judging what happens at home.

Games to Help Pupils Make Links

Games like 'finding bundles of three' (Figure 9.6) help pupils to make links. Making links and identifying why things are part of a pattern are important scientific skills. This type of learning is active and requires the pupils to be engaged in their learning. There are a number of three's that are easy to spot and are about where materials come from. The finding bundles of three activity helps to expose misconceptions, e.g. some pupils are not aware that cotton comes from a plant and in fact suggest that: 'Cotton comes from a cotton wool, it is like a sheep but it does not live here' (Year 2 child in urban school). The solid, liquid and gas state of water is easy to spot. To provide more of a challenge, pupils could be asked to spot other gases or to identify three solids. Pupils' talking in science lessons is often an underrated activity that needs a higher profile in many classrooms.

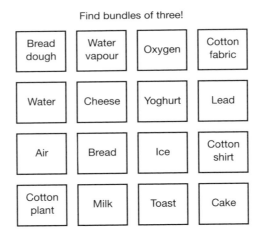

Find bundles of three!

Bread dough	Water vapour	Oxygen	Cotton fabric
Water	Cheese	Yoghurt	Lead
Air	Bread	Ice	Cotton shirt
Cotton plant	Milk	Toast	Cake

Figure 9.6 *Bundles of three*

Pupils can also make links by playing 'odd one out' (Figure 9.7). It is important to start with a number of real objects with young pupils so that the pattern can be found and increasing or decreasing the number of items with older pupils depending upon the links that can be made between them. There is always a need to use real objects until the middle of Key Stage 2, after that just providing the words and letting pupils spot the odd one out adds to the challenge.

Figure 9.7 *Odd one out*

Pupils of different ages and ability tend to choose different objects as the 'odd one out'. The object chosen by pupils of course will depend on their previous knowledge and understanding of the properties of materials. For example, some younger pupils may select metal 'because it made the light bounce', whilst most primary-aged pupils are likely to select wood 'as the rest will change state'. Metal might be selected 'because it will conduct electricity', and 'because it is magnetic'. An adult learner might select metal, as 'it is not made of more than one type of element', whilst another might suggest metal as the odd one out because 'the rest have carbon in them'.

Whilst games can be made from everyday resources it is important to ensure that knowledge learnt through games is scientifically correct, as pupils will remember both the activity and the learning. It is also important to remember that some questions in science can have more than one answer. For example, the terms predator, consumer and carnivore could all be given by pupils as the answer to the question 'What do you call a fox in a food chain?' However, the term predator is the only truly correct one as although all predators are carnivores not all carnivores are predators. Consumers also include herbivores and again are not all predators. This is important and should be encouraged through such discussions, a clearer understanding of the correct meaning of scientific terms can be developed.

Whilst it is possible to teach this information by rote, for many pupils it will only last in the short-term memory. Able pupils will be able to regurgitate the information for a limited amount of time, but the use of rote approaches can lead to confusion in the less able. Learning by rote does not enable the link to previous experiences and the pupil makes little sense of the learning. As a result they can know less and be more confused than they were before teaching.

Providing questions where the pupils select the answer will also help to expose pupils' misconceptions. Again, here the idea is that the pupils should play for short amounts of time, e.g. in starters or plenary or whilst waiting for lunchtime or assembly. When selecting questions it is important to include some of the common misconceptions. The question 'What are the incisors for?' had pupils suggesting B from the following:

A – to cut the food

B – to stop the food from falling out of the mouth

C – to tear the food

D – to grind the food

Again it is not just the right answer that is important, but *why* it is the right answer. Questions should be posed about why the pupils selected this answer and why the other answers are not right. In mathematics there has been an emphasis on asking pupils to explain how they worked out the answer, that the answer itself was not the only outcome of the learning but the strategies adopted for solving the problem were also important. This emphasis is also important in science so that pupils are not just asked to learn the right answer and accept ideas without being asked to articulate why they are right. Later in a pupil's science education this ability to justify beliefs will be even more important, and fundamentally this is what science is all about. The famous scientists who struggled to develop the immense body of knowledge that is known today had to be able to justify and convince an often sceptical public that their ideas were correct.

Whilst challenges are an effective learning approach, so is presenting information in different formats to ensure that pupils are able to transfer knowledge and understanding from one context into another. The example of a challenge in Figure 9.8 has gaps that need to be completed. Other cycles in science could also be used to challenge pupils' understanding. Just turning the arrows the other way round has dramatic effects with some pupils, as does presenting the same information as a linear flow chart. Altering the format of all work is strongly recommended, as pupils need to be made to think.

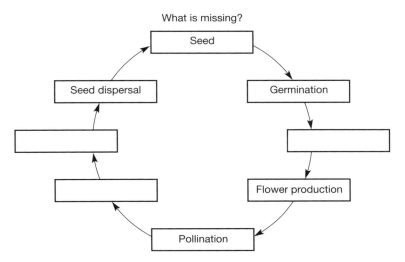

Figure 9.8 *Life cycle of plants*

Playing 'twenty questions', another popular game from the past, can provide challenge and help pupils to ask effective questions. These are the questions that will identify an object as quickly as possible. To play 'twenty questions' pupils have to ask questions to which the answer can be only 'yes' or 'no', but if they state an object (guess) and it is not the right answer they lose a life. Lives are also lost if the question cannot be one to which the answer is 'yes' or 'no'. After playing this game regularly, and by 'losing lives', pupils stop thinking about trying to guess the item, e.g. 'Is it a pencil?' and start to think of key questions that will help in all circumstances, e.g. 'Is it alive?' or 'Does it breathe?' The more experiences the pupils have, the more the focus shifts towards scientific words and questions. These skills are vital if pupils are really to understand sorting and grouping, and classification, all of which are key scientific skills. They are also used when making dichotomous keys a skill that some pupils find difficult.

There are also commercially produced board games and true/false games as well as activities that enable pupils to act out elements of science. The possibilities are unending. Whilst not all lessons should be game related, elements of the games discussed in this chapter will benefit different learning styles and some games-related activities should be built into the science teaching in each half-term. The most important criteria as to whether a game should be used at all relates to the learning intention of the lessons. If the learning intention can be met through a game approach, then deciding which game is the next decision along with knowing what the pupils will learn as a result of this game. Games are not the panacea to poor science teaching and should only be used in appropriate amounts to develop skills and understanding. The starter games can have the greatest impact as they get pupils motivated to learn, while in the plenary they enable learning to be consolidated. Some games are ideal during the main teaching section of the lesson for groups or specific individuals. However not all science lessons will follow a three part format and games might occur in the odd five minutes at any time of the day or week.

Summary

This chapter has shown the positive role games can play within a well-planned scheme of work. Not only can such games be motivating and enjoyable for pupils and their teacher, but they can also effectively reinforce important aspects of learning. More specifically, the games presented have been justified in terms of how they can help in the development of scientific vocabulary alongside knowledge and understanding of science. Importantly, the chapter has shown how games can be used to expose and deal with pupils' misconceptions.

One important aspect running through this chapter is the importance of pupils being provided with regular opportunities for discussion and collaboration. The importance of pupils engaging in collaborative work cannot be overemphasised, especially as many school science policies have this as a stated aim. The pupils of today will be growing up to work in a world where, if knowledge is needed, the Internet will provide, but group working and collaboration will be the skills most used on a day-to-day basis.

The final word on games is that there are many still to be invented, modified or rediscovered that will improve science teaching and pupils' learning. Enjoy!

CHAPTER 10

Organisational issues

Hellen Ward

Introduction

This chapter focuses upon the organisational requirements for science teaching. The organisation of the pupils, the equipment and the activities will be discussed as these will affect the learning outcomes provided for the pupils. Various groupings and organisations are possible and the ones selected will rely in part on what is to be taught but also have an impact on the resources available, as well as the confidence and experience of the teacher. Resources and their storage also have an impact upon science teaching and some ideas are suggested. The chapter concludes with issues related to health and safety.

Groupings

The ideal grouping of pupils is dependent on the learning outcome expected. If the pupils are to learn how to read a thermometer, then the groupings must enable all pupils to have access to a thermometer and appropriate media to measure. If the resources allow, this could be accomplished with all pupils working independently, but other grouping might enable resources to be more carefully managed and to provide opportunities for turn-taking and to enable ideas to be reinforced during group discussion.

As the focus of science teaching is upon learning and not just coverage, the activities provided are as important as the seating arrangements. Whilst it is common practice in coverage models to use 'drill' and worksheets, pupils are given greater opportunities to learn about science when they work in pairs or in collaborative groups on interesting activities. Most learners remember more and make a greater number of links when discussing ideas and debating issues. When the ideas and views within the group differ, more discussion occurs and as a result more opportunities for learning are provided. Equipment choices will also impact upon grouping, for example, digital microscopes enable sharing of experiences and lively debate to occur whilst manual microscopes can only be operated by one person at a time.

Individual work is appropriate for mind maps, free-range concept maps or for the development of some basic skills. Pupils should always be encouraged to record and communicate their own findings with differentiation by resource, support or outcome. This enables all pupils to 'download' their experiences, which is needed if links are to be made with previous learning experiences. Downloading, unlike copying off the board, requires some independent thought and participation by the learner.

Paired work is needed for activities requiring more than one pair of hands. Making circuits, dissolving sugars or testing parachutes are difficult for lone workers. Working in mixed ability pairs allows a 'less literate' pupil to focus on the task rather than on written recording or the reading of instructions. Most illustrative work can be undertaken in pairs and these activities work poorly with a group of larger numbers due to limited table space and opportunities to access the equipment, with some pupils taking the role of bystanders or 'on-lookers'.

While pairs of pupils are effective in many situations, when equipment and resources are limited or a complete investigation is planned, groups of three are more appropriate. Triads work very well for complete investigations because of the opportunities provided for the pupils to take different roles. The roles of observer/measurer (the eyes), recorder (the scribe) and tester (the doer), are taken in turn by each pupil in the group, enabling three readings to be taken and allowing all pupils to participate. The most able infants pupils can record all the results whilst the other pupils can just record their own.

Groups of four need to be handled carefully as pairs or a group of three and a 'lone child' can form. Groups of more than four rarely work, unless the focus is on drama or discussion, due to the limited number of roles possible. A larger group of five or six mixed ability pupils is successful for KWHL grids or debating activities as a wider range of ideas is provided. The problem with larger groups is the dominance of a single pupil, or pupils sitting back and watching as there is little for them to do. In primary education the average group size is six, which is too large for most activities that are undertaken, and smaller groups are needed if pupils are to learn. Large groups also have the added disadvantage that all the questions and ideas pass through the teacher with them controlling the debate. This issue does not only relate to science teaching and can be overcome by passing a small beach ball/bean bag from pupil to pupil allowing only the pupil with the ball/bag to present their ideas along with their evidence for these. The ball can only pass between pupils, who may have the same or contrasting views. This activity needs to be handled carefully with younger pupils, and pupils need to be taught how to debate and discuss their ideas. It also requires the pupils to listen to each other and not just wait for the ball/bag to state their own idea, so real listening skills are needed.

Although the number of pupils in a group is important, the composition in terms of gender and ability also needs thought. Grouping is dependant upon the personalities of the pupils, how they interact as a unit along with the teaching style of the teacher. Friendship groups are often of mixed ability and provide support in some cases and distraction in others. Ability in science is not the same as being numerate or literate and, if Isaac Newton were in school today, he may not have found his way into the top set! Although mixed ability grouping counteracts this, science ability groups are also needed to enable pupils to progress. If the tasks are really literacy lurking in science lessons then the scientifically able will not be challenged.

For investigative work mixed ability, single gender groups support all pupils. When mixed gender and same ability pupils were placed together the result for the pupils, and teachers, were not as effective. The most able pupils who were put together argued and could not decide upon a focus, whilst the less able pupils demonstrated clear patterns of 'learnt helplessness'. Mixed ability groups gave peer support. For equal opportunity reasons single gender groups give all pupils opportunities. In mixed gender groups the boys collected all the equipment but were then unable/unwilling to work with the girls, who often became the scribes. Grouping is a skill for the teacher who may need to alter the groups until supportive working groups are found. There will also be some pupils who find these skills hard and will need to be moved from group to group so that no one group is less successful every time.

Whilst the pattern for investigative work seems clear, it is not for other types of science. With the majority of science being composed of a range of illustrative and basic skills, lessons grouping needs to be flexible with the composition and size of the group determined from the outcomes of formative assessment.

Organisation

There are many different types of organisations possible for teaching science and all have advantages and disadvantages. Organisation of pupils' learning should principally depend upon what the pupils are to learn. The type and amount of equipment that is available, time allocated, health and safety implications, pupils' prior experience of the aspect of science and their group work skills should be considered. Organisation choice should primarily suit the learning needs of the pupils but might be selected for real (or perceived) practical constraints

All organisations are variations on the whole class or small group theme. Whole class organisation (Figure 10.1) is beneficial for introductions to lessons or for lessons where all the pupils will be carrying out the same activity at the same time. Whole class is often used when sharing science books, for demonstrations and in the plenary. Small group work is suited to situations when the pupils will be working on different activities, whether that is as a circus or when only one group of pupils is carrying out a science activity.

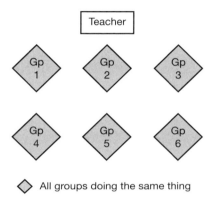

Figure 10.1 *Whole class organisation*

Whole class organisation, working with the class as a unit, does not have to be 'chalk and talk'. With the introduction of interactive whiteboards, lively whole class starters using secondary sources are possible. It is also beneficial to use a range of artefacts, discussions and pictures at the start of the lesson in a whole class setting. The advantages of whole class organisation are that the learning can be set within a familiar setting, aiming for all the pupils to be involved. There is an apparent classroom control and the intention that the pupils will be able to share ideas. In a whole class setting there are opportunities to demonstrate particular equipment or aspects of subject knowledge, and control over progression and continuity is provided. However, there are disadvantages if this organisation lasts for the whole of the lesson and is directed from the front with no involvement of pupils as individuals. When the whole class is taught as a whole it is difficult to ensure that all the pupils listen and are on task, differentiation is only possible by effective questioning. Pupils can be relatively passive in their learning, and there is little equipment needed so the pupils will not be given opportunities to develop basic skills.

Setting the same activity for all the groups at the same time, with groups all undertaking the same practical has an advantage in that pupils can be clear about the task set as only one activity is explained. Pupils are able to work at their own level, and interest is gained due to the practical nature of the task. The equipment is the same for each group so organisation is simplified and differentiation by outcome or support is possible. In the plenary there are opportunities to share experiences, although this sharing of ideas is limited by the amount of 'new' information to share. Lessons planned in this way can promote progression and continuity, but only for the class as a whole. The disadvantages of this approach are related to differentiation and resources. With all groups undertaking the same activities, matching this to the individuals is difficult and, although the equipment is easy to organise, the demand is high, as each group requires the same equipment. Planning the first lesson in a series using this organisation enables initial assessment of pupils but the success of this organisation is dependant upon extension activities and support.

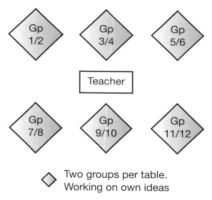

Figure 10.2 *Investigative work*

Small group independent enquiry, also known a 'child centred' investigative work, (Figure 10.2) enables pupils to raise their own questions and carry out the whole process of investigating an idea. The advantages for the pupils include motivation, differentiation and the development of group work skills (attitudes). The composition of the small groups enables the needs of individuals to be carefully matched. Thus progression of the pupil's own skills is more likely and the opportunity for shared learning is enhanced. The demands for equipment are great and can be complex. Undertaking this organisation requires mental agility and some form of scaffolding for pupils. This organisation improves with pupil and teacher experience and confidence.

The organisation, known as the 'circus' (Figure 10.3), where pupils work on different activities throughout a session, or over a number of sessions, provides many advantages. The pupils experience many related activities providing opportunities to develop skills and understanding. Interest is maintained as time

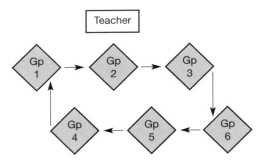

Figure 10.3 *The circus*

on each task is limited and the intense practical nature provides opportunities for group work, skill development and immersion in an aspect of science. 'Circuses', however, do have some key disadvantages. Differentiation is by outcome or support and it is not possible to have progression between the activities provided, as all pupils will work around them in a different order. The pupils undertake the different activities at the same time, and expectations and outcomes of individuals have to be carefully monitored, particularly for those pupils requiring support. Ensuring that all groups finish in time to be moved to the next activity can be problematic. However, with clear instructions and time checks it can be operated successfully. By the very nature of the organisation there are high equipment demands and this can be difficult to arrange. Even with all these issues taken into account, it is a method preferred by many pupils, and circuses in the areas of forces, sound and light seem to work successfully.

Thematic group work (Figure 10.4), where all pupils are studying science but are not all undertaking a practical science activity, is becoming more popular. This approach is beneficial for the introduction of key skills or ideas and, as one group of pupils is focused upon, their understanding can be assessed and future

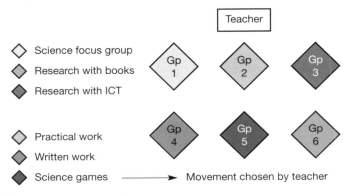

Figure 10.4 *Thematic group work*

learning planned. The focus group offers the opportunity for high quality inter-action whilst all the other activities can be set within a context or theme. The disadvantages depend upon the progress made by the pupils not in the focus group. These issues have been overcome in literacy and numeracy teaching by making pupils more independent in their learning. The key to success is the chal-lenge and quality of the independent activities. Although time-consuming, to enable all the pupils to experience all the activities, and problematic from a dif-ferentiation angle, it is a useful organisational strategy enabling the integration of secondary sources and ICT throughout a unit and supports situations with lim-ited equipment.

A worryingly common feature of primary science teaching is teacher demon-stration with the support of a chosen few pupils. There appears to be apparent control over progression and behaviour, and little equipment is needed. Exciting and interesting experiments that pupils could not undertake independently can be shown, although, in practice, demonstrations are often of everyday activities that pupils are very capable of undertaking independently. The disadvantages of this method far out weigh any advantages, as demonstrations are 'hands off' experiences. Opportunities for differentiation are reduced to teacher question-ing, which when undertaken within a full-class demonstration often result in low quality recall. Opportunities for pupils to develop skills are limited and gaining an insight into pupils' attainment is a challenge. However, demonstra-tions are excellent when carried out by visiting science theatres and groups, as these are one-off exciting events that motivate and inspire.

The science table with an interactive display that challenges pupils to under-take practical tasks is an organisation rarely used. The pupils in groups (or pairs) visit the table throughout the week engaging in a mixture of child-initi-ated activities, exploration and illustrative tasks. The activities are controllable and changed weekly to engage and motivate pupils. If this method is the only approach to teaching then progression is slow. Assessments are straightforward as few pupils undertake the activity at any one time; but teaching time needs to be allocated for this. Time is needed for instruction giving and for a plenary and the timing of these important activities is problematic. Equipment demands are few in terms of quantity, but high in terms of quality and varia-tion of experience provided over a half-term. The isolated nature of the activities, with limited opportunity for the pupils to share their experiences and the difficulties inherent in planning for individuals, make this a difficult organ-isational choice. Although more common in Early Years settings, this organisation has value throughout all stages of education if it is provided in addition to other approaches.

Integration (Figure 10.5), where science is one of many tasks available to the pupils to select at different times of the day or week, lost favour with the introduction of primary strategies. Operated effectively in Foundation Stage classrooms, pupils select from a range of teacher-directed and child-initiated activities throughout the day and week. The approach enables flexibility of time and resources, differentiation by task, progression and assessment. The focus is clearly centred upon the pupil and their learning, and the adult takes a facilitator role. The approach requires some direct input and expedition with follow-up activities and resources planned in advance. This method requires very careful planning and accurate record-keeping, ensuring that pupils do not produce inadequate work in order to progress quickly to another activity. This factor is not unique to only this organisation but needs careful monitoring. The equipment demands, although very varied, are reduced as only one group is focused upon science at any one time.

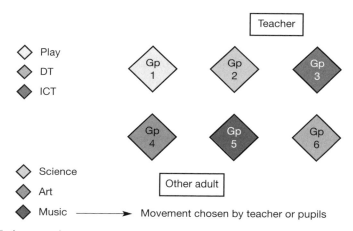

Figure 10.5 *Integration*

Individual learning programmes are now viable with the development of computer technology. The programmes allow pupils to work through levels and experience 'virtual' science activities, with some systems also enabling assessments to be stored. Using this approach it is technically possible to match the activity directly to the needs of the pupil, giving complete differentiation, progression and continuity. However, the limited opportunities for sharing ideas, for group work and for the manipulation of real resources and equipment are clear disadvantages. The approach does not develop basic science skills or reinforce the understanding that science activities do not 'always provide the same answer'. Although clean and easy to operate, it somewhat misses the point of what science is. Not all pupils learn effectively using the non-linear learning associated with computer-generated activities, and these activities should enhance but not replace traditional practical science. Although very sophisticated, using this new technology may actually only provide an electronic workbook, which is a criticised mode of learning.

Using a range of organisational approaches within science teaching is the most effective way to maintain interest and promote learning. Starting some lessons with a whole class format where pupils' ideas are elicited and written up on the board, as the ideas held, is a very effective. This can be followed by group practical tasks focused on collecting evidence, followed by a whole class discussion to evaluate the original ideas. At this stage some of the pupils' original ideas are no longer viable; they do not have evidence to support them. These are removed, leaving some to be challenged again. This cycle of elicitation of ideas, testing to gain evidence and evaluation might occur more than once in a lesson.

The important thing is to change the style and format of the lesson; too often the three-part lesson imposed by strategies has gravitated to science lessons. Some lessons may last for a morning whilst others might have many small starters, practicals and evaluations contained within them. Lessons using a circus organisation will look very different but it is this difference that will awake pupils to learning and perhaps make them more enthusiastic.

Regardless of the organisation method selected, good science should have an opportunity to discuss findings and conclusions; 'hands on' is not successful without some element of 'minds on'. With science being taught in short afternoon sessions, effective elements of science are being lost through tidy-up time. It is important to provide opportunities for pupils to explain what they have seen and understood; this occurs in the plenary. Whilst this whole class forum is the favoured option, only using 'show and tell' approaches will not enable pupils to develop real understanding. Having a quality conclusion to the lesson requires detailed planning and imagination at the planning stage. Using a range of dance, dramas, tape recording or mock television news reports alongside more traditional methods enables the plenary to be more meaningful and enjoyable for the pupils. A good plenary enables the next steps of learning to be planned, but might not occur only at the end of the session.

Whilst the focus upon what the pupils are to learn is the key factor in organisation selection, previous experience of group work will have an impact upon learning. Pupil behaviour, real or expected, plays a large part in organisational choices. The issue of control is made more difficult by whole class demonstration with limited practical experience, as there is little to motivate the practically orientated pupils. However, rushing into group work with full availability of all the equipment is not the answer, as pupils will have no experience of how to use this equipment or work with each other. Building up the pupils' confidence and discussing expectations both of ways of working and outcomes are needed. Pupils are who have been too directed lose the ability to think for themselves. Symptomatic of this is the low-level questions pupils ask related to 'underlining titles', 'collecting resources' and 'where to write on the page'. However, careful grouping of pupils with clear practical activities followed by meaningful recording and discussion enables pupils to learn science in a controlled and supported way.

Resources

The management of resources differs from school to school. The decisions taken depend on the amount in the budget, the number of classes and the status of science as a subject in the school. Whilst there is no one way to organise science resources, there seems to be some ways that are more efficient. Successful systems generally have the following characteristics:

■ The resources have been audited.

■ There is an up-to-date resource list including pictures and the number of each item.

■ There is a clear storage system with some type of coding.

■ There is a method of communicating shortages between teaching staff and the co-ordinator.

■ Systems are in place to deal with 'one off' resource issues.

■ Storage is arranged both centrally and in the classroom.

Resource Auditing

Identification of the resources into those that are essential (E), desirable (D) and additional (A) is a good starting point. Essential items are investigative equipment in class set quantity, including thermometers, timers, stopwatches, measuring cylinders, scales (preferably digital), magnifying glasses (of various magnification,) force meters and mass carriers. Whilst it is essential to have a range of ICT sensing equipment, some hand-held sensors for light and sounds would be desirable. Digital microscopes and digital cameras in multiples are desirable but having one of each is essential. The judgements will depend upon the school and are subject to change with changing technology and innovations. Although commercial games develop vocabulary, these are desirable items as they can be made; however, it is more difficult to make working thermometers.

Resourcing science has been a challenge and with changing national expectations schools have equipment which is old and unused in addition to new resources that are no longer in the central store. Resource amnesties work effectively.

Storage systems

Colour coding of the boxes and trays helps with storage and retrieval as does having a picture of the item on the outside of the box alongside its name. Storing all associated equipment in the one area denoted by a one colour tray/box or colour spot also adds order.

Ordering the equipment in associated sections makes more sense than an alphabetical list; for example, resources for measuring distance, resources for measuring forces, resources for work in the environment. Having resource files in each classroom enables pupils to select their own equipment and exposes them to associated vocabulary.

As there are no 'fairies' that tidy stock cupboards, storage ideas that are effective at point of use in the classroom are needed. If everything is just piled into a box then there will be chaos, but if equipment is placed in labelled boxes or bags within larger transparent trays or boxes, sorting and tidying begins in the classroom. Devices that enable pupils to collect and return their own equipment within the classroom do not have to be complex. In electricity, hanging crocodile clips on wire coat-hangers makes storage easy while enabling pupils to be responsible for collecting and returning their own equipment. Placing electrical equipment in a large toolbox with each section labelled has made storage, collection and replacement of standard equipment easier to manage. Making appropriate resource choices initially is important, i.e. appropriate voltage bulbs of 3.5 volt, rather than 1.5 volt provides a longer lasting resource with less blown bulbs in the classroom. Using 4.5 volt batteries, which stack, rather than 1.5 volt cells enables easy storage and equipment that works when required. When buying from catalogues, if the item it is not as expected then sending it back is the correct option.

If equipment is not easy to access or replace then this will contribute to non-practical science lessons. However there will be occasions when equipment turns up after the lesson has finished. This equipment is then left in the classroom, placed somewhere else, or slipped on a shelf between boxes for someone to find later. Thus effectively removing the item of equipment from the school stock and enabling its use by other teachers and pupils. Acknowledging that this is an issue and providing a labelled box (Figure 10.6) to put the equipment into is one solution. Science teaching assistants can replace these in their correct box. The use of science teaching assistants is increasing, with larger schools have more than one.

Figure 10.6 *Resource label*

Shortages

Consumable items are as important as hardware and a budget is needed for replacement batteries, bulbs, sugar and food substances throughout the year. All substances including sugar and salt must be labelled, and chemicals which could cause problems if inhaled, ingested or touched should be risk assessed and locked out of harm's way. The common peanut can cause problems for some pupils and copper sulphate crystals are poisonous if ingested.

Communication strategies that enable information to be transferred without the need for a face-to-face meeting are ideal, as even with the best systems there will be shortages. How the shortages are dealt can make the difference between effective and non-effective science teaching. A whiteboard and pen in the science area, for people to write up requests and suggestions is successful (tie the pen securely to stop it from walking!) as is sending an evaluation sheet to all teachers at the end of the unit of work. However, asking for contributions from colleagues is only successful if action is taken as a result.

With careful planning it is possible to borrow certain large pieces of equipment that will only be used once or twice per year. Local secondary schools can help and this provides additional opportunities for cross-phase liaison.

If practical science is to occur regularly, then equipment is vital. Science boxes in each classroom to augment the centrally stored resources are ideal. These can contain a range of items such as magnets, magnifiers, mirrors, torches, tape measures, thermometers, pipettes and syringes. In the Early Years such boxes enable child-initiated activities to occur. At the end of Key Stage 2 the equipment in the class box can include items that would promote additional experiences, for example neon bulbs, for the gifted and talented pupils. At all ages the equipment can be tailored to provide interesting and fun activities that link science with their everyday life. Providing one item of interest for the class each half-term is also effective.

Resource selection needs to include all teachers, as choice is valuable in all areas of learning and motivation is linked with this. A request list in the staffroom enables ideas to be shared, raises awareness and promotes interest, all of which result in more active science lessons, as teachers are more willing to use equipment and games selected themselves.

Health and Safety

Health and safety comprises two aspects: first, the role of the teacher and, second, the role of the pupil. Initially it is expected that pupils will follow instructions from the teachers to control the risks to themselves and others. This develops to being able to use equipment and materials appropriately and take action to control the risks.

It is often assumed in primary schools that health and safety is a matter of common sense. The Association of Science publication called *Be Safe* is specifically for primary schools, and was provided by most local education authorities for all their schools. It was prepared in consultation with HMI and the Health and Safety Executive. *Be Safe* sets out in a very clear way the main aspects of safety advice and guidance which are needed for teaching both science and technology at Key Stages 1 and 2. The layout includes guidance on activities and resources that are unsafe but also goes on to suggest alternatives to enable good teaching and learning to occur. The other main health and safety body is an organisation called the Consortium of Local Education Authorities for the Provision of Science Services (CLEAPSS). More than 95 per cent of the education authorities in England, Wales and Northern Ireland are members of this organisation. The function of this body is to support the teaching of practical science through a range of publications and provision of in-service training for teachers and technicians. They run a helpline as well as a web-based service (www.cleapss.org.co.uk) and they will respond to queries from science co-ordinators.

While common sense generally is a useful starting point, sometimes common sense is not enough, as what is commonly thought to be dangerous, such as the use of cardboard insides of toilet rolls, may have little risk in real-life situations, whilst objects brought in from a 'pound' shop without the appropriate kite marks could be dangerous when used in the classroom setting. The issue of the cardboard tubes from toilet roll tubes is an interesting one as it is one of the items most teachers state are banned. The suggestion is that children could catch salmonella from the handling of these tubes. Although opinion is divided on the matter, CLEAPSS do not believe that there is any evidence of problems with the use of the rolls or that pupils would be exposed to any higher level of germs than in ordinary day-to-day living. The CLEAPPS are more concerned about whether pupils wash their hands after the use of the toilet and if anybody checks that they do. However, some education authorities and headteachers and governing bodies banned their use and if the governing body and employers have banned the use of cardboard rolls, then teachers in those schools are not at liberty to use them.

Science should be fun and interesting for all pupils, and recommendations by both safety organisations are that risk assessment should be undertaken, but that 'over caution', making risks out of areas of no risk, will lead to limited practical opportunities for the pupils. The use of certain types of batteries for circuit work is often debated. Again it is important for teachers in schools to have an understanding of their local perspectives. In some schools the use of these items is banned. The use of rechargeable batteries is generally not recommended for use in practical circuit work due to the likelihood of them becoming very warm. However, they are perfectly safe for the use in Roamers or other equipment where the batteries are sealed from the pupils. Small 9v watch batteries are not recommended in school due to the dangers of them being inhaled or ingested, and car batteries are on the 'not recommended' list. Whilst daffodil bulbs are poisonous if eaten, digging them up from the school grounds just in case a pupil should eat one is taking things to extreme.

Risk assessments should be carried out by teachers to ensure that they are aware of the risks and hazards associated with everyday activities. All activities should be checked and risk assessed when undertaken for the first time. A simple and working definition of hazards and risks is:

A *hazard* is a potential source of danger.

A *risk* is a situation involving the exposure to that danger.

The hazard is the cause of danger, for example, with boiling water the hazard is the scalding that could occur and the risk would depend upon how much danger the pupils would be exposed to. If the kettle (only a potential hazard if it is full of boiling water which could scald) is in the staffroom, the exposure to pupils in the classroom is non-existent. However, if a kettle or jug of hot water is brought into the classroom this changes the exposure and, dependent upon the number of supervising adults and the age of the pupils, the exposure (risk) might be judged as too high. However, some teachers would risk assess this activity as safe.

Hazards can be defined as high, medium or low and in the classroom situation a high hazard is one that will cause long-term damage. Medium hazards could be considered to be those which would be uncomfortable and might need some medical attention, but have no great likelihood of long-term effect. A low hazard is something that has a limited effect. The same ranking is also applied to risks. If the event is likely to happen (high exposure to danger) this would be judged as a high risk activity, whereas a low risk activity will be one that in normal everyday occurrence or barring 'an Act of God' would not actually happen. Once the hazards and risk have been identified then a risk assessment can be undertaken. These can be formal or informal depending upon the requirements of the school or LEA. Some example are given below.

- *Boiling water in a kettle.* The hazard would be defined as high but the risk would be dependent upon, how and where the boiling water was located. The hazard will always be high but, depending on exposure, the risk could be low (e.g. a demonstration with the pupils seated a considerable way from the kettle and with more than two adults in the room.) In many schools the risk assessment is clear as a temperature of water up to 60 °C and no hotter is allowed.

- *Cutting up batteries.* The cutting up of batteries is a high hazard activity, with the chemicals inside causing damage to the skin. It is difficult to cut open batteries without cut fingers or hands. As it is difficult to make the risk less than high, this activity is a high hazard and medium to high risk, and is one that should not be undertaken. If pupils will benefit from seeing the inside of batteries then local secondary schools have models encased in plastic.

- *Opening fireworks.* Obviously a high hazard activity with the dangers of burns and blinding and, ultimately, death. The risk of exposure to danger in the classroom is high, with the electrical equipment in most classrooms being able to generate a spark. Resulting in a risk assessment of high hazard and high risk, again this is not an activity to be undertaken in primary classrooms. This is where common sense does not prevail as one teacher used common sense to argue that it was an interesting activity for young children to see and as there were no matches in the classroom there would be no risk of the firework going off.

It is important to take a balanced view with health and safety and to risk assess activities to identify a potential hazard and to evaluate the actual risk of that harm happening, then making decisions based on clear evidence. This evidence may change slightly from year to year with different groups of pupils but fun and interesting activities should be created whilst making sure that health and safety issues are taken into account.

Health and safety assessments are written into many schemes of work. However, if teachers want to undertake more innovative and interesting activities in more creative ways, then all practitioners should be able to risk assess. Whilst caution should be encouraged, real life is waiting outside the safety of schools and this should be taken into account. Banning the use of glass items when glass is found everywhere in everyday life is short sighted. Health and safety education is also about teaching pupils to deal with everyday life. If glass is broken outside school then the danger to them could be greater because of the lack of experience and exposure. In classrooms pupils will not be involved in the cleaning up of glass and the teacher will know to wrap the glass in newspaper and to then place it in a bag and not in an ordinary classroom bin. Discussing these features with pupils helps make them safer in real-life situations.

This second aspect of health and safety, that of teaching pupils to identify the hazards and risks is important. Using an everyday setting to start the process is helpful, and thinking of the hazards related to skateboarding works well. The process starts with a discussion about the hazards (dangers) of skateboarding. These hazards are then graded according to the impact of hazard using a scale of 1 to 3, with 3 being very hazardous and 1 being of limited danger. Skateboarding attached to the bumper of a moving car is a high hazard activity (3) whilst using the skateboard on a play area is safer (1). Pupils should be challenged to reduce the exposure to the danger – the risk – i.e. if a helmet is worn then the exposure to the danger is reduced. If a skateboard is used at night on a busy main road the exposure to the danger is increased.

The aim is not to worry pupils into thinking that living is a totally unsafe activity; but even the cutting of paper with a pair of scissors has some risk associated with it, if concentration is lost, if it is done while running around the playground, etc. This enables pupils to realise that they have some control and are able to make decisions that have a bearing upon things that happen in their lives. Once pupils have an understanding of hazards and risks and how these can be judged, these skills should be transferred to investigative activities. Introducing this from Year 2 upwards, at some point throughout each unit of work, enables pupils to meet the requirement of recognising the hazards in living things, materials and physical processes, and to be able to assess risks and take action to reduce risks to themselves and others.

Summary

Effective science teaching requires teachers to use many different organisational types and groupings. Some suggested groupings and organisations have been presented with the advantages and disadvantages for each. There is no one way to teach all lessons and a variety of groupings and organisations is recommended. Changing the format of lesson and pupil grouping has been suggested as a vital way to maintain interest and promote motivation. Health and safety is important, especially as society on the whole is becoming more litigious, but this should not be used as an excuse for boring lessons. If all lessons follow the same format and pupils are required to absorb information rather than generate their own ideas and understanding of science, then it will continue to be a subject that leaves learners cold. However, if the emphasis is on the pupil and their learning, pupils of today may turn into the scientists of tomorrow.

Glossary of Terms

In order to ensure consistency of use of terms within the book and also to ensure that the book is read with understanding the following terms are defined.

Basic skills: these are the science process skills that include observation, and other skills that start with simple comparisons that later lead to standard units of measurement. For example measuring temperature first by comparing samples by touch and later using a thermometer.

Children: will be used when there is a wider issue under discussion.

Experiments: these are scientific procedures designed to demonstrate a known fact in the classroom. Experiments are used to prove what is happening in a practical situation. These are often misused in primary education.

Exploration: where children are given the opportunity to explore (play) with objects in their environment. Exploration is considered to be an important aspect of learning for most people at all stages of education and beyond. Therefore it relates to the whole age range and adults. The purpose of exploration is to allow time for observation and for pupils to become familiar with objects and to raise questions about the object. This is important both for skill development and the development of understanding.

Exploratory skills: these are the skills developed during exploratory work. These include observation, questioning, pattern seeking, causal relationships (i.e. cause and effect), comparisons and use of vocabulary to describe and explain.

Illustrative work: here, provided practical work may include factors to vary and change, but the teacher makes the choice of these. Pupils have no choice. These types of practical work are vitally important because they provide the opportunity for pupils to learn important skills or procedures and also provide the opportunity for the practical work to illustrate some aspect of knowledge of science.

Investigations: these provide pupils with the opportunity to undertake complete or whole investigations where there are identifiable opportunities to:

- identify factors and change variables

- identify factors or variables to measure or observe

- allow choice by pupils.

Learning intention: the aim of the lesson. This is what the pupils are to learn and should include knowledge, understanding, skills and procedures and attitudes in science.

Learning objective: what pupils will do in the lesson.

Learning outcome: specifically what pupils are expected to learn in the lesson. These are used for assessment purposes and differentiated for different groups/individual pupils.

Practical work: pupils being provided with the opportunity to have 'hands on' practical experiences. These fall into a number of categories:

1. Investigations

2. Illustrative activities

3. Experiments

4. Basic skills

5. Observations

Programme of Study: from the National Curriculum and *Curriculum Guidance for the Foundation Stage.*

Pupil: will be used throughout to describe children in the context of teaching.

Scheme of work: often termed 'medium-term plan'.

Scientific enquiry: is an umbrella term that encompasses many aspects of activity. National Curriculum (2000) denotes scientific enquiry as planning, obtaining and using evidence along with an understanding of the nature of scientific ideas. Exploration, illustrative and investigative activities would fall into this.

Scientific process: process and procedures used consistently when pupils are engaged in aspects of scientific enquiry.

Structured play: is where a situation is set up by the teacher and where the teacher or classroom assistant or other adult asks focussed questions to meet planned previously identified possible learning outcomes. There is a flexibility of approach where identified objectives may or may not be met in the session. At the end of the activity the teacher/other assesses what learning has taken place against possible learning outcomes and records these with any collected evidence to support the conclusions reached.

Unstructured play: is where the teacher or other adult provides equipment, but there is no clear outcome intended. The role of the teacher here is to stand back from the activity and watch for more informal opportunities to take learning on from a child-initiated starting point. Learning is assessed on an individual basis.

References

Assessment Reform Group (ARG) (1999) *Assessment for Learning: Beyond the Black Box*. Cambridge: University of Cambridge, School of Education. http://www.assessment-reform-group.org.uk

Assessment Reform Group (ARG) (2002) *Testing and Motivation*. Cambridge: University of Cambridge, School of Education.

Black, P. and Wiliams, D. (1998) *Inside the Black Box: Raising Standards through Classroom Assessment*. London: King's College School of Education.

Bruner, J. and Haste, H. (1993) *Making Sense – the Child's Construction of the World*. London: Routledge.

Camp, L. and Ross, T. (2000) *Why: Meet Lily, the Little Girl Who Always Asks Why*. London: Picture Lion.

Clarke, S. (2001) *Unlocking Formative Assessment*. London: Hodder and Stoughton. Department for Education and Employment (DfEE) (1999) *National Curriculum: Science*. London: DfEE .

Clarke, S. (2003) *Enriching Feedback in the Primary Classroom*. London: Hodder and Stoughton.

Department for Education and Skills (DfES) (2003) *Excellence and Enjoyment*. London: DfES.

Foreman, J. (2002) 'An investigation into the impact of role play on children's attitudes and learning in primary science lessons'. Unpublished MA (Ed) dissertation, Canterbury Christ Church University College.

Gardner, H. (1993) *Multiple Intelligences*. New York: Basic Books.

Goldsworthy, A. (1997) *Making Sense of Primary Science Investigations*. Hatfield: Association for Science Education.

Harlen, W. (2000a) *The Teaching of Science in Primary Schools (3rd edition)*. London: David Fulton.

Harlen, W. (2000b) *Teaching Learning and Assessing Science 5–12 (3rd edition)*. London: Paul Chapman Publishing.

Johnson, G. (1999) 'Kidney role-plays', *School Science Review*, 80: 93–7.

Johnson, J. (1996) *Early Explorations in Science*. Buckingham: Open University Press.

Kolb, D.A. (1984) *Experiential Learning: Experience as the Source of Learning and Development*. Englewood Cliffs, NJ: Prentice-Hall.

Office for Standards in Education/Her Majesty's Inspectorate (OfSTED/HMI) (2002) *Ofsted Subject Reports 2000–01*. London: HMI. www.ofsted.gov.uk

Office for Standards in Education/Her Majesty's Inspectorate (OfSTED/HMI) (2003) *Ofsted Subject Reports 2001–02* London: HMI. www.ofsted.gov.uk

Office for Standards in Education/Her Majesty's Inspectorate (OfSTED/HMI) (2004) *Ofsted Subject Reports 2002–03* London: HMI. www.ofsted.gov.uk

Parliamentary Office of Science and Technology (POST) (2003) *Post Note Primary Science*. September. London: POST.

Pollard, A. and Twiggs, P. (2000) *What Pupils Say: Changing Policy Practice and Experience*. London: Continuum.

Qualifications and Curriculum Authority (QCA) (1998), *Schemes of Work*, London: QCA.

Qualifications and Curriculum Authority (QCA) (2000) *Curriculum Guidance for the Foundation Stage*. London: QCA.

Qualifications and Curriculum Authority (QCA) (2004) *Standards at Key Stage 2 English, Mathematics and Science 2003*. London: QCA.

Qualter, A. (1996) *Exploring Primary Science and Technology: Differentiated Primary Science*. Milton Keynes: Open University Press.

Science and Technology Committee (2002) *Science Education from 14 to 19*. July, House of Commons/Stationery Office ISBN 0 21 500422 1.

Sherrington, R. (1998) *ASE Guide to Primary Science*. Cheltenham: Stanley Thornes.

Smith, A. (1999) *Accelerated Learning in Practice*. Stafford: Network Educational Press.

Smith, R. and Peacock, G. (1995) *Investigation and Progression in Science*. London: Hodder and Stoughton.

Taylor, A. (1997) 'Learning science through creative activities', *School Science Review*, 79: 39–46.

Van Ments, M. (1983) *The Effective Use of Role Play: A Handbook for Teachers and Trainers*. Revised Edition. London and New York: Kogan Page.

Index